TWELVE
CLEAN
PAGES

Published by:
bel esprit books
P.O. Box 821801
N. Richland Hills, Texas 76182-1801

ISBN 978-0-9835907-1-2

Publisher's Cataloging-in-Publication data
Maples, Nika.
    Twelve clean pages / Nika Maples.
    p. cm.
    ISBN 978-0-9835907-1-2
1. Maples, Nika. 2. Cerebrovascular disease --Patients --United States
--Biography. 3. Stroke --rehabilitation --Personal Narratives. 4. Quadriplegia
--Biography. 5. Systemic lupus erythematosus --Biography. 6. Teachers --Texas
--Biography. 7. Christian biography. I. 12 clean pages. II. Title.

RC388.5 .M27 2011
362.1/1681/0092 --dc22   2011907780

Cover design and interior page layout by theBookDesigners
Front cover photograph: © 1985 Gilstrap Photography
Back cover photograph: © 2011 Sugar Maple Portraits

Printed in the USA

TWELVE
CLEAN
PAGES

A MEMOIR

NIKA MAPLES

bel esprit
books

Fort Worth

To
CCM,
heroine of my heart.

No discipline seems pleasant at the time, but painful. Later on, however, it produces a harvest of righteousness and peace for those who have been trained by it. Therefore, strengthen your feeble arms and weak knees. "Make level paths for your feet," so that the lame may not be disabled, but rather healed.

—Hebrews 12:11–13

PROLOGUE

My maternal grandfather drove a bootleg liquor truck when he was sixteen years old. As one might expect, he garnered many friends as he rocked along Georgia's winding roads, his prohibited cargo jostling under ropes and a tarpaulin in the rusty truck bed. They called him only by his surname, Cotton.

Sometimes I wonder if he thought of his mother. Maybe he remembered her hands as he drove on bright days, windows rolled down, the Southern sun freckling his arm. The same rays that smiled on him had bitten mercilessly into his mother's flesh. Every day, deep auburn blisters bore into her hands, corroding the skin on her fingers. Lesions continued to spread onto her arms and sun-sensitive face until misery kept her in the shadows. Her tongue swelled, filling her mouth. It was dementia that turned the last lock on her desolation. Already imprisoned inside a wasting body, she spent her final days in a mental institution.

Pellagra, a cruel illness that swept the South at the turn of the century, had jimmied the back door of her house like an insidious intruder. She, nor anyone else, could secure the area. Pellagra continued creeping into home after humble home, harassing town after tormented town. An estimated three million Southerners developed the disease between 1907 and 1940. And one hundred thousand died.

Over time, scientists connected pellagra with the corn-based diet of those living in poverty. Dr. Joseph Goldberger conducted experiments on volunteer inmates in Mississippi prisons to prove his revolutionary theory that pellagra was merely a dietary deficiency, not a bacterial infection. The idea was so simple that some people were hard pressed to believe it. But the evidence spread out like a clean tablecloth: when fresh meat, vegetables, and milk were introduced into their diets, patients soon recovered. In fact, the deficiency could be reduced to *one* particular vitamin. Word spread quickly; this mysterious and sometimes terminal illness could be cured with adequate doses of niacin—vitamin B3.[1]

The news was too late for my great-grandmother. In the year of that landmark medical discovery, the family received a telegram announcing her death. Her husband succumbed to a heart attack a few years later, leaving my grandfather entirely responsible for himself in his early teens. Determination and a mere eighth-grade education were his only possessions. With funereal tears still fresh on his face, he formulated a plan. He knew he must transport liquor during Prohibition in order to stay alive.

Alone.

1 Office of History, National Institutes of Health, "Dr. Joseph Goldberger and the War on Pellagra," by Alan Kraut, PhD, http://history.nih.gov/exhibits/goldberger/index.html.

My paternal grandfather grew up in Texas. His middle name, Freeman, was an almost fairy-tale nomenclature for a boy who led the unfettered life of a hobo in the early nineteen hundreds. As a sixteen-year-old runaway with only a seventh-grade education, he jumped trains from north Texas to New Mexico and back to Texas again, working ranches, digging wells, and sleeping in rickety boxcars along the way. His shoulders became stronger than the rails he rode.

He had left home suddenly. His mother had died in the flu epidemic of 1918. Then, his father remarried. This new wife treated my grandfather harshly at times, commanding him to fetch logs for the fire and using the very wood he brought to whack his legs. His father, a blacksmith, also heaped a myriad of cruelties on him. One day he asked my young grandfather to pick up a horseshoe—moments off the anvil. Men from town, accustomed to leaning against the walls of the shop to swap full-bellied stories, cackled at the boy's gullibility. He dropped the hot horseshoe from his burned hand and looked up in time to catch his father laughing. My grandfather's skin may have been seared, but not as acutely as his heart. The next morning, he told his family that he was walking to the service station to hitch a ride into town. Instead, he hitched a ride as far west as he could go.

Alone.

Both of my grandfathers learned the depth of the valley. As adolescents, they walked through the single pain that every child fears. They were alone. Both men would warn you with solemn tenor that calamity is no respecter of age. They trudged onward, but their early disappointment did not make for gentle terrain.

Life's landscape held tragedy, sudden and wild. Each tenacious step took courage.

And so it is with us.

Our mornings and evenings are a repetitive and intimate dialogue that invites us to hope, to bring our whole hearts to the table to devour another day. But just when we begin to enjoy the breakfast conversation, Life pushes back in his chair and comes across the table for our innocent throats. He tackles us to the floor, sometimes with such force that we hesitate to pull ourselves up, lest he subdue us again. After such a blow, it seems impossible to move forward. From that moment, we struggle to convince ourselves that morning is a holy invitation to live better, to breathe more deeply than yesterday. In spite of yesterday.

Maybe even because of it.

My brother uses an apt label for people who have survived some great hammering blow of trauma or distress. He calls them the Initiated. He suggests that the Initiated always can communicate most easily with their kind. The language of loss is common, although the actual events surrounding each moment of devastation may not be. One who has faced Initiation often refers to his life as a timeline on which the chronology seems to extend in opposite directions from a central, shattering event. There were the experiences that took place *before*, and there are the experiences that have taken place *since* the Initiation.

The Initiated can speak to one another intimately because they come from the same place. They have learned to operate from new priorities, new motivations, new perspectives. Disillusionment has made a completely new person out of each of them. Wherever they were born originally, now they hail from a harsh countryside, and traveling its stone-sharp valleys has yielded too many wounds to count. The Initiated recognize one another as fellow expatriates. They have been cut deeply, and deep calls to deep.

Yet, how breathtaking the realization: one who has experienced a hollowing heart-wound possesses an increased capacity for joy. Those who have *not* been hurt can merely cup joy in their hands; the inner well is only so deep. By contrast, the Initiated know a great deal of pain, and as a result, a great deal of joy. It is almost as if they have been carved out. They do not just cup a hand to receive joy; their entire being becomes a vessel. A fresh beauty born of Life's brutality. Able to feel, to receive ... more. What is merely ladled for others is pitcher-poured into them. This is not because they have earned more joy, but because they are thirstier for it.

Two men fall to their knees at the edge of a river. One has crossed the lush hill country. The other, a scorching desert. Both desire the cool water's refreshment, but only one drinks with his soul.

Part 1

ONE 1

1

March 1994

THE SIRENS WERE SINGING MY NAME. I could hear them coming for me, calling to me, crying out as the ambulance spun around the street corner. Another moment might have been too late. Tires ground to a halt at the curb, and the mournful whine died. Red beams flashed into the bedroom.

Two paramedics barreled through the front door, and my mother ran to them. I started vomiting. Lying on my back, I could not raise or turn my head to spit the refuse out. I could not open my mouth. Trying not to inhale, I waited in agony.

This is it. Right now. This is the end. Right here.

At twenty years old.

After resting a gurney near my feet, the EMTs dropped on their haunches; one knelt close to my face. His words were long and wide with a Texas accent, and he talked to my mother over his shoulder casually, as he assessed my motionless body.

I wanted him to move faster. The other paramedic mentioned, in polite tones, our freshly painted front door. They had pushed into the bright red stain as they fell inside.

"Y'all should have put up a Wet Paint sign," he said amicably. It sounded as if he were showing the scarlet smear on his forearm to her, chatting as if he had come to call on a family friend.

"Oh," she said, noticing.

The paramedics knew what they were doing. As long as they could distract my mother, she would not be looking at *me*. They were trying to prevent her from descending into panic while they rescued her only daughter, a task they were not sure they could do.

I screamed inside, *Pay attention to me! Look in my mouth! Look in my mouth! I am about to choke!*

When I started heaving again, vomit erupted from my nose and forced my lips apart. They all quieted suddenly, and the EMT nearest me quickened his pace, turning my jaw, scooping tongue and throat with gloved fingers. Both men lifted me onto the gurney, and we were out the door and into the ambulance in one brilliant motion. One of the men instructed my mother to drive her minivan when she tried to climb in beside me.

"You're gonna need to follow behind us, ma'am."

She rushed off, and the paramedic jumped up after the gurney, carefully maneuvering in the cramped space.

"I want her with us ...," I said with labored breath.

"It's not like the movies, kid," he said, warning me. "This is going to be a rough ride, but I've got ya." The back doors slammed, and he squeezed in at my side.

"I heard ya hate needles," Texas said, chuckling. His kind

voice smiled down on me. "Then the *last* thing you want is for me to stick ya while we're in this racing vehicle of mine. So let's make ourselves a deal, huh? You stay awake for me, and I won't stick ya. Lemme hear you talkin'. C'mon now."

"Hold my hand," I whispered.

"Atta girl." The ambulance lurched forward, and he clasped my hand in both of his, holding tighter as we gained speed. "Here we go."

Our street was luminous in the night as the fire engine, ambulance, and minivan pulled away from the house. My seventeen-year-old brother, Mark, sped into the neighborhood just then and whipped his steering wheel around to join the swift convoy on the tail end. When the emergency vehicles entered the near lane on the main road, the fire engine broke away from the corps, and the ambulance quickly took the lead with lights only.

Mark had not expected this. He knew I was getting worse, knew I needed to get to the hospital immediately, but when he turned onto our street and found it blazing like a carnival fairway, his spine stiffened. Employing a last-ditch logic, he convinced himself that it was not a life-or-death situation until they fired up sirens along with the lights. He willed himself not to feel fear.

I could not hear the screaming traffic, because my right ear was ringing at an alarming volume. It was both a high-pitched squeal and a low buzz. My senses were dulling; there were only the paramedic's voice, my thoughts, and the awful noise in my ears.

Tex took away his hand when I became very still. We were two minutes into the ride.

"Stay with me, kid. I don't want to have to stick ya. Talk to me. Talk to me." He rapped his knuckle on my sternum.

"Hold ... my ... hand."

"That's it! Stay awake. Keep talkin'. As long as you talk, I can hold your hand. No more fadin' out on me. Got it?"

My eyes had not opened since my mother had made the 911 call. The hospital was twenty minutes away, in downtown Fort Worth, and the longer we drove, the more peaceful I became. A soothing sensation eased through me. I melted into a consciousness of one solitary breath at a time. Concentrating, I took another. And, carefully ... another.

"I told ya to stay with me!" He knuckle-knocked my chest again. It was a hard jolt, jerking me from the warmth into which I had been sliding. Now the buzz seemed to sizzle out of my right ear and down my entire right side, burning my arm and leg. Nerves crackled under the skin. A fiery hum lit each joint. There was a distinct line down the center of my body. On the left side, I felt normal. On the right, aflame.

"You gotta keep talkin' to me!"

Everything I had been thinking and wondering slowed. All thoughts coalesced into a liquid unit of information, like a swelling drop of water on a rainy window ledge. Just a singular sentence in my head: *This is what it feels like to die.*

No life-flashing-before-my-eyes experience. Just emptiness. No wishes or promises or bartering away. Just serenity. The paramedic had been right. This was *not* like the movies. I knew I was dying, and I was not afraid. Only the essential continued to occupy my thoughts.

A second bubble of information: *I want someone to hold my hand.*

"Hold ... my—"

"There ya go! Wake up, now!" As I came to the surface, I realized that he had been shouting at me. He pounded my sternum with greater strength now. "Stay with me! C'mon, kid! C'mon!" He struck my chest until his voice cracked, and I heard him choke with feeling.

Suddenly he stopped.

The back of the ambulance was still, hushed. He leaned close to me. Warm breath faintly brushed my cheeks. I could tell he was looking directly into my eyes, as if my eyelids would flutter open by the sheer force of his will.

We sped along in silence, face to face.

Then he whispered, "Can you see them, kid?" Compassion rose in his voice. It was a final, quiet plea. "Look. Can you see their faces? *Look* at them."

I took a slow and shallow breath.

"Look. Can you see them? Those are the people who haven't had a chance to love you yet. Please, don't take ..." He paused.

I inhaled.

Regaining his voice, he said, "Don't take their chance away, kid. Look at their faces. Don't take their chance away."

Exhale.

Then, like breaking clouds, my austere thought pattern parted, and I could see face after smiling face in my mind. None were faces I recognized. I wanted to tell him. I wanted to tell him that I *could* see their faces, but I made no sound.

The ambulance tore into the emergency drive, and my new friend expertly released the bed, throwing open the back door simultaneously.

"We're here, kid," he said.

The last drop of thought fell: *Thank you.*

My brother finally allowed himself to be afraid in the hospital elevator. He and our mother had had to hurry to catch up with the men who were running the gurney down the hallway. They all crammed in closely beside me for the claustrophobic ride up to the ICU. Breathless, Mark watched the paramedic snap his fingers repeatedly in front of my face. In a fevered attempt to rouse me, the EMT was leaning over, talking loudly, and urging me to stay awake. Mark could sense our mother's desperation as she stood vulnerable and voiceless at his arm.

I do not remember anything about shuttling into the hospital or taking the elevator or entering the ICU in a blistering rush. By then I had lost consciousness.

2

SHADE IS NOT EASY TO COME BY IN FORT WORTH. The sun is king here. A Texas August infamously burns the backs of young swimmers and turns seat-belt buckles into branding irons. Our summer inferno is unrelenting.

There was a time when I was not afraid of the sun, but that was before my Initiation. Now I cannot remember how it felt not to flinch from the anxiety a bright sky brings, not to feel a tremor in my bones on a cloudless afternoon. I was only twelve years old when I met the predator who would teach this fear to me.

The word *lupus* is Latin for "wolf." Systemic lupus erythematosus is an autoimmune disorder shrouded in mystery; it turns the body against itself like an unwilling soldier in a twisted civil war. The immune system battles organs and connective tissue as if they were foreign bacteria or viruses. In this sense, I am my own enemy. Lupus derives its name from the scores of patients who develop discolored blotches and wounds on their faces, which reminded doctors of wolf bites long ago. The nickname for those scarring rashes—spreading on either side of the nose with the symmetry of crimson wings—is "butterfly rash."

But a butterfly is beautiful, benign. Lupus can be fatal, depending upon the organs it targets. Heart, lungs, and kidneys ... *all* are at risk. So the image of a wolf seems more accurate to me.

There is not a cure for lupus, but there are times when the patient experiences months of relief and remission. Things can change suddenly, however, even in a matter of minutes. Frightening internal shifts are not visible to others. Lupus patients lose count of how many times they hear comments like, "But you were just fine a minute ago" or, "You look like you are doing all right to me." Loved ones are astonished by how quickly lupus awakens, but they are no more astonished than the lupus patient himself. Lupus reveals no rhyme and reports no reason.

Lengthy periods of dangerous lupus activity are called flare-ups. Some painful flare-ups come as surreptitious assaults, but during times of great stress, they are predictable. Part of lupus is extreme sun sensitivity that incites flare-ups in varying degrees in the hours or days following extended ultraviolet exposure. There are times when I have been in the sun too long and I can feel a slight and slow searing inside of me, almost like I am being cooked alive. A smoldering sensation spreads on my skin, especially my cheeks. My hands and fingers weaken. Each thought feels thick and sluggish; confusion takes me captive. Usually, there is a hat in my bag and a parasol in the trunk of my car. It is not safe to be outdoors until the sun sets. Tethered to an umbrella or to night, sometimes I feel like I am one part Mary Poppins, one part bat.

At the point of my pediatric diagnosis, the initial display of lupus was extreme arthritic pain and decreased kidney function. I was losing three grams of protein a day. A renal biopsy was inconclusive. In immunology, the knee-jerk response in 1986 was Prednisone, a corticosteroid medication. At age twelve, I took the highest daily dosage a growing child should take.

Prednisone causes numerous side effects, some potentially life threatening. The comparatively reasonable side effects are hormone related: hyperactivity, racing heart rate, mood swings, insatiable hunger, acne, darkened facial hair, and a signature swollen "moon face." Pictures of me in middle school do not even look like me. My cheeks are so puffy that my eyes seem small. My smile is pinched.

Because I was disheartened about being alienated from other students due to my unattractive appearance, I reasoned with my mother that weaning off the Prednisone would eliminate some of my grief, no matter the repercussions to my health. She responded by helping me to understand the gravity of my illness and walking me through the medical literature. I remember reading those books while curled up on my pink calico bedspread, crying inconsolably. Some of the case studies included fatalities, which petrified me. One day after reading about lupus again, a realization struck, and I was startled out of self-mourning. Standing up from the bed, I closed the book. It was time to stop grieving and start surviving. I walked out of my room, my childhood ebbing behind me as I made my way down the hall. Without tears, I came up to my mother, suddenly a determined young woman.

"I will stop whining about the medication," I told her. "I would rather be ugly than dead."

She notes that my fearful outlook never returned in quite the same way.

I was positive of God's loving care at a very early age. There was never a time I did not pray to Him and adore Him. Even through the onset of my lupus, I was sure He was developing a plan for my life. Though I had some anxiety about a future with chronic disease as a bunk mate, I desired to show my complete dependence on the Lord. I was going to need Him and I knew it. I could suffer alone or suffer with a comforting Presence by my side. If I was going to be in pain, I wanted it to *mean* something in the end.

Most people in our generation perceive hardship and misfortune as ill-timed and pointless accidents allowed by a reckless—or worse, *care*less—God. Some may view pain as a cruel, divine game.

"How could a loving God do this to us?" they cry. "Why?"

With Christ, suffering is redeemed and redefined, and there is no meaningless wound. There always is a point to it, both for us and for others, and usually it is a point of growth or a point of departure. There *is* such a thing as pointless suffering … it becomes pointless if we do not grow. Spiritual growth and progress only occur when we willingly give our suffering lives to the Lord. For it is there, on that altar of sacrifice and surrender, that we are truly Initiated. From that sharp point—from the tip of Abraham's blade—we embark on an epic voyage. We leave our own tame plans and paths to faithfully walk in the Lord's wild and mysterious will for our lives. We never return to the same inexperienced perspective.

Let it absorb into your heart, to heal you like balm: our pain means something. And by His grace, our surrender is changing us or taking us somewhere. Every hurt can have a positive purpose—no matter its source. Some trials come directly from the Lord as discipline. Some are dealt by the enemy. Some are the painful result of another person's free-will choice. Some are the fallout of our own free will, our sin. Some result from being in the wrong place at the wrong time in this crazy world.

All trials are allowed by God. None are surprises to Him. And none are beyond Him. He can employ any circumstance for our spiritual good. This difficulty becomes our discipline. That ache, our education. God recycles—repurposes—everything so that no pain is wasted. We must trust.

In the book of Genesis, Joseph shares a tearful reunion with the very brothers who meant to leave him for dead in a ditch years before, and as they embrace him, they tremble, tortured by remorse and terrified that he will avenge himself. He holds more power and has more resources in Egypt than they can dream. It would be easy for Joseph to bring a punitive disaster upon them that will last the rest of their wretched lives. But from the depth of his abiding trust in Jehovah, he begs his backstabbing brothers not to worry; he will not repay their betrayal.

And he forgives them.

"You intended to harm me, but God intended it for good to accomplish what is now being done, the saving of many lives," he tells them. In other words, *God's plan is bigger than you, dear brothers.*

Hundreds of years after Joseph reunited with his dysfunctional family, Jesus receives news that his beloved Lazarus is desperately ill. He responds in an eerily similar way.

He assures, "This sickness will not end in death. No, it is for God's glory so that God's Son may be glorified through it" (See John 11:4).

All of this is bigger than you think. It's bigger than you.

Obviously, there was a redemptive reason underlying Joseph's slavery and imprisonment. And there was a *point* to Lazarus's illness. Their adversity was part of a plan that is still unfolding— a plan that only God comprehends. That same precious plan is bigger than us, dear friends. Much bigger than our plans for ourselves.

There were only twelve years before illness found me, only twelve pages left clean in my life. They represent the time before I opened this sketchbook heart to the hand of a brilliant Artist— the Author and Perfecter of my faith. The pages turned since have been ruined gloriously.

On each day is an illustration of His grace.

Life is never about our comfort. It is always about displaying God. Humanity is the canvas on which Christ's glory is painted. We gasp when we realize that sometimes the paint is pain.

And sometimes suffering is the brushstroke.

3

THREE

SOLEMNITY FOLLOWED ME INTO THE WATER on the night I was baptized. When my father raised me up from the baptistery that Wednesday night, he was so proud of his young daughter. For a second after I rose, we stood, beaming at one another. I was never more secure in his love for me. But even with the safety of his arm around my shoulders, there was worry. My bottom lip throbbed. Running my tongue over it, I could feel the swelling. When I reached up with dripping fingers, I found it tender to the touch and too warm.

Turning my face toward family and friends, I experienced a frightening dissonance. Supportive people surrounded me, yes, but I understood keenly that I was taking my first steps on a curious path I would walk with God *alone*. The Christ journey had begun. On the evening of my baptism, I believe a passage cleared that would have remained closed, had I opted to endure illness in isolation rather than in partnership with God, for His glory. That early decision, that new pathway, changed the direction of my life. He would not guide me away from suffering, but straight into it with the ferocity of faith.

In the beginning, my adolescent mind kept hoping that lupus would go away. *Maybe a cure is around the corner,* I imagined. Only gradually, there developed a deep acceptance that sickness might always be a part of who I am, like my hazel eyes or my sense of humor.

Acceptance does not necessarily mean resigning oneself to an undesirable situation. Acceptance is controlling our responses to uncontrollable circumstances. I did not resign myself to chronic illness. I simply controlled my response.

If this *is the case, then I will* ...

Two conscious decisions helped me to accept life with lupus. First, I decided to *live* until I die. Second, I decided to *laugh* instead of cry.

One night, a dream taught me even more about the empowering act of acceptance.

I am in an orchard. I am a little girl with long brown hair, tied back with a white ribbon. I am wearing a white dress with a wide sash; the skirt is hemmed in lace. I eat the apples, play hopscotch in dappled sunlight, and sing into a sweet breeze.

Then a Wolf saunters through the orchard gate and leans low to the earth when he sees me. His lip quivers, baring an inch of pale pink gum line. Saliva drips from his teeth. Fearful, I try to lure him out of the trees, but he attacks, tearing at me, leaving me as a ragged, bloodied mess.

While he is distracted or disinterested, I run from the Wolf, stopping only when I am safely outside the orchard gate. I stand there for a long time, watching him lick my sticky blood from his claws.

At dusk, I realize that I cannot reach the fruit inside the fence to feed myself. So, gazing up at the rich trees, I resolve that the Wolf and I will have to share the orchard somehow.

Somehow.

Then, an idea. I quietly and purposefully walk through the gate, singing. I sing to the Wolf until he falls asleep. While he sleeps, I pick the fruit as fast as I am able. I keep singing. I am resolute ... and just soft enough. I sing continually. Carefree melodies are no more. I sing for strength.

I will spend the rest of my life keeping the Wolf asleep with my lullaby.

When I awoke, I understood. I share my fruitful life with lupus, the Wolf. As far as it depends upon me, I must sustain his slumber with the songs of a joyful heart. Those, he can neither tear nor take.

After the steroid treatments in middle and high school, my kidney function improved. I began to feel so much better that I often forgot I was sick. Some new friends did not have an inkling about that weaker part of who I am. I avoided any conversation that might reveal it. Wellness, even the illusion of it, was irresistible to me.

At the small Christian school I attended, students had ample opportunities to become involved. And so the level of my participation at church and at school became almost comical; I tried everything. My agenda was a kaleidoscope of commitments.

But Danger kept himself on the schedule too. The busier I became, the less I paid attention to my health. Weekends were too tightly planned to include adequate rest. I ate junk food at lunch and after school. I pressured myself to stay involved in just as many fun activities as the teenagers who were not sick. An adolescent idea of what was fair stayed just beyond arm's reach. Sometimes I thought I could outrun illness and catch up to my idea of fairness. I had not had a significant flare-up and had not been hospitalized since seventh grade, so I felt confident and powerful. Though I did not feel ill, I knew logically that I was going to damage my health by keeping such a frenetic pace. Still, I did not decelerate.

All the ingredients were on the stove to boil: very little rest, poor eating habits, and lackadaisical sun exposure. All I needed was an extremely stressful situation in order to complete the ominous recipe.

In the spring of my junior year, I came home to find my mother sitting on the living room couch, her eyes downcast. That night I was eager to moan to her about some boy-related frustration. She was looking at her lap, and when the front door closed hard behind me, she slowly raised her head. I jumped right into the narrative.

Well into my sixteen-year-old's saga even before I sat down, I stopped suddenly, noticing that her face was a pool with no reflection. Normally, she would have commiserated with me.

"Mother?" I stared down at her, waiting for a response.

She was silent.

"Mom?"

I waited until she began.

"It is hard for me to listen to this," she said. "There are more serious things to consider tonight, Nika."

"What do you mean?"

"Your father has had an affair," she whispered hoarsely. "He has been involved with another woman for some time."

There was no other sound in the house. I reeled, almost losing my balance. I could not manage a clear thought or sentence. Only a wordless image began to form. Of all the meaningful interactions I had shared with my father, I treasured one the most. A familiar picture of the two of us at my baptism crystallized first in my mind. At the moment of my spiritual rebirth, he had been there with me, wading waist-deep in that watery intimacy of my soul. Suddenly, I lost my breath, grasped by a great infidelity.

"But he *baptized* me!" I shrieked, tears already wetting my cheeks. "He can't leave! He can't just decide not to be a part of us! We're a family! You can't decide not to be a family!"

My mother sat, fingers worrying a tissue, letting me rage. She had known for several days and had hoped that my father would tell me himself before he left us for good. In the end, he had delegated that job to her. He had been so kind as to set an emotional minefield on our domestic landscape and then drop her in the middle of it. She could not make a move without setting off a heartrending explosion in her children.

Sometimes there is no comfort anyone can give to a child. There was nothing she could have said. When I had been told that I would face the rest of my life with a potentially fatal illness, it had not been half as difficult to process as the idea that my father had chosen another woman over my mother and another family over ours. He felt he could not stomach our family—what I considered the most precious part of my life—for one more day. I began to question everything I knew to be stable or secure. Stepping into my once warm home that evening, I had entered a cool, cavernous void. No verbal consolation could have stopped the floor from foundering beneath me.

With a damaged heart and listless spirit, I staggered to my bedroom, fell onto the quilt, and wept into my pillow. My breath shuddered until, hours later, I finally fell asleep.

And the Wolf opened his eyes.

FOUR 4

March 1994

A **WAVE OF PANIC CRASHED** on the still shores of my being. Through the red crochet of closed eyelids, I could tell that florescent lights buzzed overhead. Someone was humming and busy around me.

She flipped off the light as she left the room. It was dark and very quiet.

I tried to sit up and could not.

Where am I?

Then I remembered the ambulance ride.

This is the ICU. Same night. It has not been that long.

Outside the room, someone said "paralyzed." Another reported that my heart rate had dropped to twelve beats per minute on the way to the hospital. Twelve. I could hear the beats blipping now, low and weak, through a heart monitor nearby.

I am still alive.

The events of the evening were coming back to me. I curbed the panic this time.

Nika, go slow. Figure it out.

Starting methodically with my face, I checked my body, determining the ability that remained. Discovering that I could not open both eyelids, even with great effort, I marked off *eyes* on my mental list. Now *mouth*. My bottom lip quivered then stopped.

I just found my biggest problem.

I continued the self-assessment, trying to move both arms, hands.

My fingers, please, my fingers!

One by one, I crossed these off the list. Now *legs* and *feet*. *Toes*. No part of my body moved of my volition.

I have nothing left.

I have ...

nothing.

My father lived, and worked as an emergency physician, two hours away, so my mother called and left a voice message as soon as she arrived at the hospital on Wednesday night. Early Thursday morning, he pushed into the ICU like a sheriff through swinging saloon doors—half physician, half father. When he arrived, he and Mother began their vigil of milling around my bed, tending to every perceived need, talking to one another uncomfortably. The other patients in the ICU were sectioned off by curtains. We were in the ICU's quarantine room, which had glass walls, a door, and privacy. My family could stay with me as long as necessary.

Mark pulled up a chair and held my hand. No one knew what to say. I could not decide if it would have been more awkward to speak or just to lay there, the mute figure in the middle. Ironically, my lifeless body was the perfect metaphor and poetic representation of the members of our family: *quadriplegic.*

Four not functioning.

A nurse asked Mark to move aside, and she pulled back the pile of thin blankets, lifting a corner of my hospital gown discreetly.

"It's a Heparin shot," she said, rubbing an alcohol swab just below my navel.

Mark and Mom turned to my father for a layman's interpretation. Using a somewhat detached tone, he went into medical mode, explaining that the Heparin is prescribed to prevent blood clotting.

"She'll be getting these shots in her belly twice a day," the nurse said before leaving.

"Blood clotting?" Mark asked in my father's direction.

"Her circulation is going to be affected soon enough."

"Why?"

My father sighed. "She can't move, son."

5

WHEN I WAS EIGHT YEARS OLD, my mother gave me a peacock feather. With one look at its gilded shimmer, I was spellbound. Taking two pieces of Scotch tape, I adhered the feather to the wall above my bed, where it stayed like a prized piece of abstract art until—grievous to me—it was lost in a move, years later.

I was a senior in high school before she told me that Flannery O'Connor, the legendary Southern writer, had given the peacock feather to her.

My mother grew up in Columbus, Georgia, and in 1962, she had taken a field trip with her senior English class to visit Andalusia, O'Connor's ancestral farm in Milledgeville, Georgia. Mom remembers the stunning peacocks that roamed freely on its bright lawn. She remembers how Ms. O'Connor greeted the class with warmth and grace, even as she dragged herself heroically on crutches. The celebrated author answered endless questions about reading, writing, and her novels and short stories. Then she gave every student a vibrant peacock feather as the class departed for school. My mother saved hers for twenty-five years.

Fascinated by the feather, I dove into Flannery O'Connor's body of work, thrilling to her eloquent caricature of the Deep South and her incisive commentary on humanity's tendency to warp spirituality. I fell in love with the way she marries a character's delicate psyche to a near-grotesque experience. Her style is both rugged and raw in its splintered simplicity, like a rigid church pew on a page. Through her writing, she seemed like a woman who had offered a handshake to Life and had received a backhand to the cheek in return. Before long, I understood why.

Sitting in the library one day, I learned the cause of her death and froze, the book of literary criticism shaking in my hand. Only two years after my mother's senior-class field trip, Ms. O'Connor died of lupus. It had ravaged her body for fifteen years, leaving her to limp her last days away. Lupus was the reason for the crutches that carried her. It had rapidly taken her independence and mobility. Even as she suffered, she knew how much more damage lupus could cause: when she was a teenager, she had watched her father die of the same disease. She must have steeled herself when the Wolf came back for her too. Pure resolve allowed her to live ten years longer than her doctors' prognoses. At the time of her death, she was thirty-nine.

Part of the O'Connor tragedy is the cache of short stories forever unwritten. The Wolf snatched them from all our hands.

In memoriam, her beloved peacocks were sent to various hospital grounds and parks throughout Georgia. By the 1980s, the last of her birds perished. The irony stings. Almost all were victims of wolves and other wild predators.

I wrote my senior theme about Flannery O'Connor's work and life, like I would write a eulogy for a friend. Just knowing that she understood our shared illness made me feel as if, somehow, she knew me as few could. As I filled the pages, I felt the recognizable stiffness seizing my own knuckles. In the mornings before school, I would function somewhat normally, but painful arthritis progressed throughout the day. I could not hold a pencil by the afternoon. Relief washed over me when the final school bell would ring.

Both hands were locked in fists by evening. I found that hot water brought momentary reprieve. With the tap running at an uncomfortably high temperature, I plunged my curled fingers into the flow. The joints made a painful popping sound when I pulled to extend them under the faucet. Steam clouded the mirror until I could stand it no longer and had to pull my hand away, bloodred and only slightly more flexible. The next day produced the same routine.

Swollen lumps formed on the soles of my feet and the palms of my hands. My lips and tongue were in agony. I felt dizzy. Daily fatigue was profound. I did not tell anyone that lupus was attacking me again. Honestly, I feared returning to high doses of steroid medication. I wanted to look attractive for my senior year. A distorted appearance was not an acceptable option. *Later*, I thought. *Not this year.*

I never would have told anyone if I had not needed a physical for a college application. My father drove to Fort Worth to perform the routine examination. Because my parents were separated, but not yet divorced, at times we all talked and acted as if our family were still intact. Dad felt tremendous guilt for the emotional trauma he had caused us, but he had no intention of walking away from his new life in another city. He continued the dangerous charade of paternal participation in our family, both through occasional visits and unreliable funding. Mark and I shared a secret hope that our parents' separation might be temporary. But the truth was that my father was still cutting himself off from us. He had chosen to perform the amputation with a spoon instead of a scalpel, in the name of kindness. Our pain was not lessened by the use of a blunt surgical instrument, just prolonged.

When my father performed the examination for my college application, I tried to disguise the signs of a lupus flare-up. He listened to my lungs through a stethoscope. Though it hurt to inhale, I breathed deeply, and I told him I felt fine. Hiding a wince, I moved all my joints in a full range of motion. I was certain I was fooling him, though he squinted at me skeptically. Later, he approached me with preliminary urinalysis results and a stern expression.

"Why haven't you told anyone you are in pain?"

"What are you talking about? I am a little stiff now and then, but that's normal for me. Other than my usual arthritis, I feel *fine.*" I rolled my eyes and waited to see if he would buy my aloof act.

He scowled. "We are making an appointment with the rheumatologist this week. This is not a game; you are dealing with a serious illness here." The urinalysis was abnormal.

No one can be sure if things would have been better had I not tried to keep my flare-up a secret. There might not have been a difference if we had addressed my lupus four months earlier, when I first had felt its increased activity. The internal harm may have been done already by the time I noticed the joint pain.

It is useless to speculate. Within weeks of my college application physical, my deception was defunct. Everyone understood the critical situation at hand.

A few weeks later, I sat nervously at a conference table with my mother and father, two rheumatologists, and a nephrologist, who had examined the results of my second renal biopsy and was concerned. We gathered to discuss an aggressive and experimental form of treatment for the diffused damage the nephrologist had discovered in both of my kidneys.

Chemotherapy.

I really wanted Mom and Dad to make the decision, but when the discussion ended, everyone at the table turned to me. For an hour, I had been deluged by terrible words like *dialysis, organ transplant,* and *irreversible damage.* In order not to face those horrifying possibilities, they recommended an alternative that held equally disturbing potential. Taking chemotherapy at such a young age, they had warned me, might cause infertility, organ damage, stroke, vulnerability to infection, and an increased likelihood of developing cancer later in life. The doctors had not mentioned temporary vomiting and hair loss. Those classic side effects would seem like comic relief on such a permanent and portentous list. The other disheartening topic discussed that day was the questionable chance that the chemotherapy would be beneficial. They told us it might not be.

While everyone waited, I swallowed hard. "What ... um ... what will happen to my *hair*?" I finally choked.

"Well, while chemotherapy *is* an aggressive treatment for lupus, you will be receiving a less frequent and less intense dose than the average oncology patient would," one physician offered. "My guess is that you will not lose your hair. When receiving cancer treatments, a typical patient can expect to face a powerful cocktail of drugs. You will have one: Cytoxan. Also, cancer patients receive chemo once a week or more often for a short length of time. We are proposing a long-term treatment of once per month for two full years."

I would begin during my senior year in high school and continue until I was almost halfway through college. I tried to picture it. Swallowing again, I turned to my mother. Her strength in times of distress is her ability to remain unflinchingly calm. Ironically, if she had appeared frightened, I would have felt safe. Because she was summoning her deepest reserves of fortitude, I knew the circumstance was dire.

"You are eighteen, Nika," she said. "This kind of decision is one that only you can make for your body. We cannot make it for you."

I looked into the eyes of each physician. The nephrologist wore dark glasses, and he reminded me of the embezzlers and drug smugglers I had seen in action movies. It was an image that fit to me, because all the bad news seemed to be coming from him. He was stealing everything I looked forward to. Each severe statement carried off another crate of dreams.

I turned back to my mother and suddenly remembered my first onslaught of fear as a child. "I'd rather be ugly than dead," I had told her then. When I thought back to that day of my youthful resolve, the answer came to me: I would do it. I did not pray, nor did I ask for some time to think about it. In my head, there were dismissive answers for all the unknowns surrounding chemotherapy. If I became sterile, I could adopt children. If I became bald, I could get a wig. If I had a stroke or developed cancer ... I would deal with the rest when we came to it. I wanted to keep my kidneys.

"Fine," I blurted. "Fine. I'll do it."

6

SIX

I WROTE IN MY JOURNAL, "First day of chemotherapy: no big deal."

That morning my mother drove me to an oncology clinic instead of to school. Each woman in the waiting room wore a turban or a wig. I disassociated myself with every last one of them.

My situation is completely different, I convinced myself.

The whole place was silent, except for muted noises in the receptionist's area. Almost immediately, I noticed there was no coughing or sneezing, no kids pulling at their mothers' purses. The waiting room was like a vacuum. When the receptionist slid open the glass on the counter, all the breathable air sucked through the window into her section of the office.

She checked off a name on her clipboard before she spoke. We stared at her, waiting.

"Nikki? Nikki Maples?"

I stood at attention like a dutiful military draftee, accepting my call to what I knew would be certain injury. I intended to go to the treatment room to receive the chemotherapy alone, so at my insistence, my mother stayed in the waiting room, a magazine in her lap. I doubt she read a word.

The dreary treatment room had about seven blue vinyl recliners arranged in a half-moon. Three women were leaned back, eyes closed, draped to the chin with light blue blankets. Other than their heads, only their feet were visible. A thin, transparent snake coiled upward from somewhere underneath the blanket to a bag on a stainless-steel stand. Passing a few open chairs, I chose the recliner closest to the wall. I walked quietly so that I would not wake the sleeping women.

The oncologist had discussed an implanted port during my consultation a month before. He had suggested that delivering the chemotherapy directly into the bloodstream through the port would be much better for my circulatory system than repeated intravenous lines through the back of my hand over the course of two years. I had refused the procedure stubbornly. A port implanted under the skin sounded permanent to me; although he had insisted that it is removed safely after treatments end.

Oh no, I told myself. *He doesn't get it. This season of sickness is just temporary. I will be well again very soon.*

A cheery nurse in purple scrubs tapped the back of my left hand with two gloved fingers for the first of many times in that room.

"There you are," she muttered toward a vein in my hand and then inserted the IV needle. I followed the tube from my hand to the plastic bag, filled with brackish liquid.

She asked me if I wanted a soft drink or a magazine. I shook my head and thanked her, thinking, *This is not a place I plan to get comfortable, ma'am. Let's just get it over with.*

Snapping off her gloves and turning back to the counter behind her, she resumed the report she had been writing on a clipboard when I had approached her earlier. A *Gilligan's Island* rerun played on the television bolted to the wall. The volume was too low to make out the characters' lines, but the regular, soft gales of fake audience laughter joined the symphonic rhythm of the patients' careful breathing like a macabre opera.

The first drop of Cytoxan was cold. A spider with frozen legs had entered my wrist. He led an arachnid army, and I could feel the quick and quiet scratching of their frigid march up my left arm. Then the drug hit my heart. When it did, an explosion of ice spiders skated throughout my body. Instantly, I was shivering.

I whispered to the nurse that I would like one of the blankets that the other women were using. She glanced at my goose-pimpled legs. I had worn shorts and sandals on that gorgeous April day. A few minutes later, I begged her for a second blanket.

My mother walked in after fifteen minutes. She could not stand it; she had to see how I was doing. I was relieved to see her but did not have the energy to explain all that I was feeling. My skull felt waterlogged, as if I had inhaled a swimming pool. I rested my heavy head on the vinyl recliner and inhaled slowly.

The other women were not asleep, after all, I mused. *Perhaps they could not keep their waterlogged heads upright. Maybe they were meditating. Maybe they were holding on for dear life.*

I could not stop the room from whirling and pitching, so I closed my eyes. The spiders skittered on ice under my skin.

For a few days, I felt fine. I went back to school, and all my friends asked about my chemotherapy treatment. I told them what the doctor had told me, that it was not a relatively large dosage, and that I would probably not lose my hair or experience extreme nausea. No big deal.

The objective of chemotherapy treatment is to carefully and deliberately poison the patient's biological systems. Everything starts to die a slow death. Just enough of the body dies to kill off what is not supposed to be there, like rampant cancer cells, or in my case, a rowdy immune system. To me, one obvious kink in the plan was that my immune system was not comprised of undifferentiated tumor cells, nor was it an intruder to exterminate, but *really me*. My physicians wanted to desecrate it in a controlled way, leaving as little as possible in order to maintain my breath and heartbeat. The idea behind using chemo for lupus is that when new blood cells generated, they would function properly, in defensive—no longer offensive—mode.

When I agreed to take chemotherapy, I did not fully comprehend the fact that the IV would be a pistol full of poison, aimed directly at my heart. Every cell within me was kicking and flailing against a toxic suffocation.

All systems screamed in unison during the physiological nadir. The nadir occurs when chemo causes the body to take its deepest swing toward death. I experienced my first nadir two weeks after treatment, in the middle of the night. I was not fully awake and into the bathroom before I started retching violently.

My mother heard me and came running. I could not stand, so she tried to take my temperature from where I knelt in front of the toilet. We had a minute between my heaves to take a reading on the thermometer: 106 degrees Fahrenheit.

I held a bucket on my lap as we drove to the emergency room. Still in pajamas, I lay my sweat-sticky forehead against the cool car window for some relief from the fever. I vomited in the bucket the whole way.

I was in the hospital for a week. My white blood cell count had dropped much lower than doctors anticipated. The nadir was not supposed to be this severe.

All the nurses wore yellow paper face masks, and I did too. Several school friends visited, bringing snacks. Families from church sent flowers or plants. None of it was permitted to come through the door. Outside, food landed in the hallway trash can, and plants stayed at the nurses' station. Every friend who came to visit me wore a face mask, gloves, and shoe covers.

After finally leaving the hospital, I participated in as many senior activities as my health would allow. I smiled for photographs, received honors and congratulations, and tried to dismiss the nagging apprehension that things never would return to normal.

7
SEVEN

March 1994

INTENSIVE-CARE NURSES TOOK VITAL SIGNS every thirty minutes. They lifted my lifeless hands. They peeled open eyelids to peer into glassy irises. They turned my body to its side every two hours. Every two hours. Every two hours to prevent bedsores. The longer a person remains immobile, the greater the likelihood that the skin will split and break open at the points of contact where the patient's heels, hips, or shoulder blades meet the bed. The healing process is garish. But bedsores might be avoided by regular changes in position, so the nurses turned and turned and turned my body. I lay on my back, then right side, then back, then left side. I endured it. My lungs were so fragile that the shift to my sides left me burning for shallow breath until the nurses turned me again. I tried to rest while I was on my back, because I knew that I would not be able to do so on my side. I chastened myself to fall asleep during those brief supine moments but never could.

Though my body was motionless, my mind was an engine with the pedal to the floor. This was because the treatment administered to me upon arrival in the ICU was massive doses of steroids: 1000 mg per day for five consecutive days. The medicine caused my thoughts to race, and I occupied myself by making amusing lists. Refusing to become morose so soon, I tried to find the humor in my situation. I reminded myself of my own long-standing commitment to deliberate living: "To live until I die, and laugh instead of cry."

Things I Wish Were Different:

1. I wish Mother would stop eating sunflower seeds within my sensorial range. Every time I hear them tinkle out of the glass jar and smell their salty sweetness, my mouth waters. MY MOUTH WATERS! Let's all agree that this is unfair.

2. I wish the room would hover at a nice, reasonable temperature, instead of rising to a microwave-frenzied heat. I am starting to feel like a bag of popcorn. Why does the nurse keep adding blankets? Wait, I get it: I look like Han Solo frozen in carbonite, so I must be cold, right?

3. I wish someone would take these extra-tight, extra-high tube socks off. The elastic band is cutting off my circulation from the knee down. BESIDES, MY FEET ARE NOT COLD (see number 2)!

4. I wish people would stop using my bed as a table. Surely this is an obvious consideration to make. The last time a doctor put a heavy book and a clipboard on my legs, it was a long time

before he remembered where he'd placed them. Meanwhile, my legs were in serious pain. It is not like I am laid out in a funeral parlor here. Show a little respect, will you?

5. I wish everyone would stop speaking to me in simple, childlike sentences. My arms and legs don't work, but my mind does. The trick is getting everyone to realize it (note to self: when you get out of this situation, Nika, remember that mental ability and physical ability are not mutually indicative).

6. I wish nurses would stop startling me awake every half hour to shine glaring penlights into my pupils. The ripping-open-the-eyelids thing? Yeah. I'm about done with that.

7. I wish Mom and Dad would stop kissing my cheeks and forehead. Really, I wish *everyone* would stop kissing my cheeks and forehead, including my old orthodontist, who seized the day and went directly for my mouth (somewhat ironic, don't you think?). It's called *personal space*, people.

8. I wish others would realize that I can hear them talking when they are standing just outside the doorway. The threshold is not a soundproof barrier of any kind. And I also know that the pronoun *she* means "me." Easy one.

9. I wish my teeth did not feel like they were covered in tiny, dirty Persian rugs.

10. I wish someone would scratch my nose.

The blankets not only added warmth but they added weight. With each passing hour, it was becoming more difficult to breathe underneath them. Finally my mother noticed the beads of sweat on my brow (I inwardly rejoiced at her discovery!) and peeled away all but one thin blanket, folded back at the waist. Even then I could hardly inhale. The sheet—only the sheet—felt like a sheet of iron, not cotton. With every breath, I consciously had to lift my rib cage. This is why breathing was so laborious while I lay on my side. My flaccid arm increased the weight I had to lift.

All of this happened over the course of a few days. If my legs, my arms, and my mouth slowly diminished to total immobility then ... I reasoned cautiously, *I think the same thing might be happening to my heart and lungs. Soon they will not move.*

No one had to tell me I was dying. But as medical professionals discussed my condition—assuming that I was comatose and not listening actively—they inadvertently did. My evolving mental lists reflected this grim realization.

Things I Wish I Had Done More Often:

1. Forgiven. No strings attached.

2. Read the Bible. Right now, the Lord is able to draw to my mind only the few verses I know by heart in order to sustain my soul.

3. Watched sunrises. There were not many mornings I had bothered to reserve a seat for the finest exhibition in the world. There is never any cost for admission. We just have to make the meager effort to show up.

Things I Wish I Had Done Less Often:

1. Held a grudge. Had I really commandeered brain cells to store negativity and resentment?

2. Pushed Snooze. Why do we waste so much of our mobility while we have it? Running, cycling, stretching, *anything* is better than laying still.

3. Watched so much TV. When I am gone, the television will not remember me. Only the people in whose lives I invested will.

If only I had a chance to live again ... I would live differently.

Training my site on a target, I aimed for twin criminals: Pride and Idleness. Dressed in unassuming clothes, they seem harmless enough. They whisper to us that they are not nearly as dangerous as Hatred, Adultery, Murder, and Lies, their vicious cousins. But Pride and Idleness are desperate for our time and attention. They follow us around, tricking us into letting go of one hour, then another, then another, then another, until we reach into our pockets and realize we have no time left to spend. Pride and Idleness are thieves. They rob us of every delicate opportunity. Will we drop another day into their dented tin cups, as if they were needy beggars rather than seasoned con artists?

Pride steals our opportunity to illustrate Christ. Because of Pride, we refuse to humble ourselves and reach out to a person who has hurt or offended us—and we should do this, not because what the other person did was right, but because what God did was right when He elected to die in their place. His choice was to forgive. Who are we, not to offer what Christ offers willingly?

Pride is the identity thief, masquerading in imposter's clothing. Pride convinces us that we are being righteously indignant. What we often call "righteous indignation" may be plain ol' Pride dressed in finery. Beware: what Pride encourages is not righteous. Behind the mask, it does not look a thing like God. When we choose to harbor a hurt or hold a grudge, we are not drawing others to the image of Christ. We are employing the familiar methodology of someone else entirely. Look closely and you will recognize the enemy.

Then Idleness steals our opportunity to spend time well. Time is the most valuable commodity on earth, because it is the only thing we can never reacquire. What Idleness takes from us, we can never earn, buy, find, or be given again. Within the stringent laws of time, there is equal distribution. We make ourselves wealthy or bankrupted in emotional resources and creativity by the way we choose to invest our individual allocation of hours. In saunters Idleness, our slick and sinister stockbroker. He convinces us that we will benefit from a little "folding of the hands to rest." That we will feel so much better if we just sit down for a minute to "veg out," watch TV, play video games, surf the Internet, update blogs, check our friends' statuses online, or read pop culture magazines—generally wasting time without engaging our hearts, brains, or spirits. Meanwhile, songs and books are not written, houses and relationships are not built, Bibles and emotions are not read ...

And the children grow up.

Idleness cackles as he walks away with a briefcase he can hardly snap shut. Bills flutter about as he turns for one last word to each of us, "You fool! Didn't you know which endeavor would pay off in the end?" His laughter echoes through our empty lives.

Many of us will find ourselves in paupers' graves, buried under a mound of missed opportunities.

I desired to change my ways right there, as I lay on hospital sheets, by inviting Humility and Diligence to have the guest rooms that Pride and Idleness had been occupying in my heart.

First, I gave Idleness a solemn warning that his days were numbered. Should I have the opportunity to move again, I would no longer *passively choose* Idleness by *not actively choosing* Diligence. I did not want my life to be characterized by a couple of hours of daily television and only fifteen minutes of daily Bible reading and prayer, if that. There were days when I spent no deliberate moments with God. It is a farce to say that I did not have time. I had plenty of it. If I watched TV at all, I had at least *that much* extra time on my hands. Television is not inherently bad, but it is a luxury, pure and simple. We watch TV when there is nothing more important to do. But most of the time, there are many things more important to do. When I was watching TV, I was not spending time most effectively. Which is not to say that there is not an appropriate time for rest. Certainly there is. Yet, how fine is the line between rest and waste.

Idleness is apathy "in action." Apathy is the opposite of a conscientious mind-set. It is indifference, lack of concern. In terms of spiritual growth, apathy seems to be the disease of the day. Unlike other ailments, an apathetic or lazy spiritual lifestyle is a matter of choice. We can do something about it. We can choose to grow. If we care enough, we will nurture our spiritual lives consistently. If we do not care enough, we will lose our past growth through the haste of every day's business, as surely as weeds encircle a delicate bloom and choke its life.

Spiritual apathy leads to spiritual atrophy, and that was a condition I was desperate to avoid. I decided that my new motto would be Cure Laziness. I did not even want to cure lupus as much as I wanted to cure laziness in myself. Lupus is beyond my control, but in matters of laziness, the healing is up to me. Yet, for obvious reasons, my battle with Idleness would have to be won much later, outside of the hospital, when I finally would have choices other than to lie still for days on end.

After addressing Idleness, I went for the most difficult and elusive thief: Pride. His presence in my life had nothing to do with the hospital or my state as an invalid. I could kick him to the curb right then and there. I would not have to postpone his eviction until a later time. Humility cannot wait. Forgiveness cannot wait.

I had to forgive my father for tearing apart our family.

When we have been betrayed or abandoned by one who had our deepest trust, we carry on our shoulders a heavy challenge to forgive. Like the myth of Atlas, we cannot drop the weight of a ruined relationship easily. To pretend that we are not carrying it, to ignore it, is to fancy ourselves magicians. No, we cannot "make it go away," because it is real. It really happened, and now we will haul around the sorry carcass of what-was until the day we die. Unless we forgive. Forgiveness is the act of setting down the burden at last. It is not as easy as it sounds. Tell Atlas, there will never be a more difficult thing to do in all the world.

My father did not expect me to forgive him. He knew how I smoldered with quiet fury. How could I prove to him I finally had let it go? I devised a plan and practiced. When my father came in the ICU one evening, he sat down and held my right hand. With all my strength, I tried to move my little finger. It twitched.

Elated, he ran to get my mother, but when she held my hand, I did not move. He took hold of it again.

"I felt her finger move! It is not just my imagination! Wait and see," he said. Right on cue, I moved it again. "There! Try again! She did it!"

My mother grasped my hand and waited again. I did not move.

"I don't feel anything."

My father insisted and took my hand a third time. "But if you are still enough, you can feel her move ..."

Again, I twitched my little finger in my father's hand.

Again, my mother felt nothing. Then he was sure it was for him.

And though I was imprisoned in my body, I was finally free.

8

SOMETHING DARK SLITHERED DOWN MY ARM. Startled, I looked quickly, but nothing was there. I shook my head under the shower stream, shaking the image from my mind. Closing my eyes for a moment, I leaned back and let the hot water run over my face.

A few seconds later, I saw it again. This time, I looked directly down to the tile floor of the shower. A small clump of hair slipped through the grate and washed away. As the water continued to pour on my scalp, another larger clump dropped and stopped up the drain. Panicking, I hurriedly turned off the faucet with one hand, clutching my head with the other. Then, grabbing a towel, I ran to the mirror to assess the damage. On the left side of my head, shiny patches of skin peeked through. On the right, it was worse.

Collecting my thoughts, I cleared the shower drain and dressed somberly. I opted to let my hair air-dry, afraid to blow more of it off and away with the hair dryer. Then I combed it with a careful hand, tossing fingers-full of hair into the trash. Once dry, my hair was passable, not nearly as spotty as it had been when wet.

That afternoon my mother returned from work before I came home from school. In the bathroom, she glimpsed the trash can, with long, tangled hair up to the brim. It took a moment before she could catch her breath.

For a few weeks, I brushed each strand with strategic vision, letting my hair swing to cover balding areas. My friends pretended not to notice the difference as I coiffed thinning locks like an airy meringue, making it seem like there was more substance than there really was. Bits vanished daily. I was molting, for heaven's sake. Sooner or later, a good-natured friend was bound to say it. I lasted another week before my best friend, Becky, insisted that it was time to buy a wig. By then, I wholeheartedly agreed.

We had gone out on a Friday night in Becky's Jeep. Her father always took the doors and hardtop off in the spring. We would buckle up tight and ride around Fort Worth with the warm wind whipping our hair like a blender. Later we joked that, for once, we should have taken my car instead.

Another friend rode along with us, so I sat in the backseat, which happens to be the hellish vortex of a convertible vehicle on a highway cruise. I felt like a pilot in a wind tunnel with an open cockpit.

When we arrived at the restaurant, I caught my reflection in the front door. The whole hair-loss experience had become almost entertaining to me. I called Becky to hurry over.

"Is it just me, or did I leave the house with a lot more hair than this?" I snickered, peering wide-eyed into the glass. It could no longer be denied.

"Dude ..." She paused, smiling. "There's only one way to say this: we gotta get you a wig."

The first wig I purchased looked ridiculous. I arbitrarily had suggested that we buy it because I was moments from crying and wanted to get out of that humid wig shop immediately. My mother and Becky brought many colors and lengths of hair for me to survey as I sat in the barber's chair in the center of the mirrored room. We stopped at only one store and stayed for fifteen minutes before I was emotionally spent.

"This is the one," I announced, standing to go. "Come on."

My real hair was light brown, all one length, and fell to the middle of my back. The new wig was dark mahogany, chin-length, with bangs.

That was my everyday wig. I wore it to my graduation ceremony, and needless to say, I did not toss up my mortarboard cap with the rest of the celebrating graduates. I was afraid my wig might fly up with it.

The second wig was worse. It had occurred to me after a few weeks of wearing the everyday wig that I did not have to be confined to one look. I could get another wig for special occasions. If you are going to wear a wig, multiple options are a bonus, right? My special-occasion wig for prom was the same dark mahogany color, but it had waist-length spiral curls. I used bobby pins to hold the curls up on the top of my head. When I left the house with my date, I felt both pretty *and* practical, because my casual everyday wig was tucked in my backpack with a change of comfortable clothes. For a second, I started to think wigs were brilliant.

Then I saw the pictures the next week. The problem was that both of my wigs were cheaply made, as far as wigs go. My mother was not about to spend money on more realistic versions. Because I had twisted up the curly tresses on the special-occasion wig, heavy seams where the synthetic strands of hair were knotted to the nylon scalp were obvious. The professional photos taken that night still make me cringe. I might as well have been wearing a Halloween wig from a grocery store aisle. I looked like one of those stuffed witches or overall-clad scarecrows that neighbors set out in a lawn chair on their porch with a bowl of trick-or-treat candy in his lap.

I suddenly became disgusted with the whole concept of wigs. The idea of shaving what was left of my real hair seemed rebellious and strong. When I had asked my mother about it, she had told me—only half kidding—that she would wring my neck if I did.

"But she's not the one tucking a sad little ponytail up under a burning hot wig," I said to myself later in front of the mirror. On my scalp, there were broad swaths of bare skin and an ever-thinning fringe of hair. I hated watching it fall out, strand by strand. I was not going to observe helplessly as chemotherapy took my hair. I would take it myself.

As soon as my mother left for work that morning in June, I drove to a cheap hair salon. Sitting in the chair, I pulled off the wig and loosened the rubber band around my scant ponytail.

"Shave it, please," I said confidently to the young woman with shears in her hand. She did not speak, but after a long time of silently staring at my head, she started to weep.

"*What* are you doing?" I turned to look at her.

"I can't," she said, signaling to the girl across the room. She pleaded to her friend, "Will you do this? I can't."

"Look, just shave it," I insisted.

The second girl shook her head. She did not have a customer.

"I can't do that either."

"What?" I threw up my hands incredulously. "I need someone to shave it, that's all. I can go somewhere else, if you want me to." I could not comprehend their reticence.

Both girls went to the back of the salon and left me sitting in the chair by myself. They returned with the manager in tow. She asked me if I was sure, *absolutely* sure, and then she shaved my scalp. There were tears in her eyes. The two girls stood and watched with hands clasped and grieving expressions on their faces, as if a vet were putting down a favorite pet.

When I went to pay, the manager would not accept any money.

"You don't owe us anything. Just go on home, darlin'."

Such a gloomy reaction was unfathomable to me. I felt exuberant. I placed the wig back on my scalp when I was in the car. It fit better, felt a few degrees cooler, and was no longer lumpy and uncomfortable. I drove straight to my mother's new office. She had left her counseling position at the private school to join a nonprofit organization that assists individuals with mental and physical disabilities in their efforts to achieve independent living arrangements.

Standing in front of her desk, a joyful look on my face, I ripped off the wig and said, "Surprise!"

I was the one who was surprised, however. She dropped her head into her hands and began to cry. My arms fell, along with the smile on my face. In all my life, I have seen my mother cry precious few times. That was one of them.

"What in the world is wrong, Mother?"

It was a few minutes before she could say, "I was not ready to see you like this. I was not ready ..."

I slapped the wig back on my bald head and drove away in a huff. It would be a long time before I understood that my illness did not affect only me.

9

FOR MY MOTHER'S SAKE, I wore the everyday wig a few more weeks. During that time, a friend and I were chaperones on a summer outing for kids living in a home for abused and neglected children. We drove our own car and met the kids' bus at a roller-skating rink.

We thought we were fantastic dancers. Key word: *thought*. We had always had fun practicing elaborate flips and twirls in our driveways. Our cooperative dream was to amaze an unsuspecting crowd. In the fantasy, all average dancers would part like the Red Sea to make room for us on the dance floor, and we would star in our own *Saturday Night Fever* moment, spinning through well-rehearsed, choreographed movements as if they were impromptu.

We were ready to try this charade on the children at the skating rink. It had worked a couple of times before. One night we even did our little number at the pricey restaurant at the top of Reunion Tower, the signature "lollipop" in the Dallas skyline. We only ordered ice water before jumping on the dance floor.

Everyone oohed and aahed. A middle-aged couple asked us if we were dance instructors who offered lessons.

We were too embarrassed to tell them, "No, we're actually in high school. We'd better hurry on home and do our algebra homework now. We don't want our mothers to find out we were here on a school night."

It was a challenge to replicate our dance on roller skates, but the kids separated, as if on cue. It was magic. They thought we were stars. They might have continued to think that, in fact. But we just *had* to show off and do the flip.

At first, neither one of us noticed. We kept on dancing until one of the kids screamed, "It's a dead cat!" and pointed to a spot on the floor a few feet from where we were performing.

The DJ ripped the record to a halt. My friend and I stopped dancing, turning to look at the crowd, at the floor, and back at each other simultaneously. I slapped a hand to my shiny scalp and gasped.

The "dead cat" was my wig.

"I'll get it. Stay here!" he ordered, letting go of my hands.

Shocked, I lost my balance. My arms fought the air like windmills. Both skates rolled out from under me, and I fell flat on my rear end.

He skated over to the cat/wig and brought it back to me. Facing our stunned audience of children, he shouted, "She's all right, kids." He dropped the cat/wig on my head cheerily and patted it a little.

"Come on back out. She's all right!"

Maintaining eye contact with the crowd, he leaned down and shot out a whisper from the corner of his mouth, "Will you *get up*, Nika?"

"I can't *get up!*" I fired back.

He looked down and saw for the first time that he had placed the cat/wig backward on my head. Long hair hung over my eyes. Wispy bangs were in the back.

I went home, knowing exactly what to do. A "dead cat" deserves a proper burial. I closed the wig in a drawer and did not exhume it again.

At other times, it was difficult to find humor. The chemo caused bleeding mouth and nose ulcerations. Exhaustion was like a lake of sludge, and I could not buoy myself up for air. No matter how long I slept, I would wake up just as tired. I vomited all the time: at school, at church, at my friends' houses, kneeling beside my car in the parking lot outside the grocery store, under the bleachers at a high school baseball game. A hurried, emergency state became normal to me: Be ready to pull over. Remain close to an exit. Make sure to note the location of the bathroom. There were days when I would not be able to get up from in front of the toilet at home for an hour at a time, and by then the carpet had carved pebblelike impressions in my knees.

Only one incident really scared me. I was getting ready for church when I leaned in close to the mirror to apply lipstick. I noticed a thin line of saliva seeping out of the left side of my mouth. My face looked droopy. I thumped my cheek with my fingers and then tried to smile. I still had feeling and movement, yet something was different.

Fear mounted as the day progressed. When I drove to church, my right pinkie kept going limp and getting caught in the steering wheel when I would make a turn. I drooled lightly all morning. With a tissue, I had to keep wiping it away. There was one moment, so quickly there and gone, when I could not remember how to take a step. I stood there, and my leg would not move. Then I was fine and walked away. Later, my arms were lethargic, and I dropped my Bible in the circular driveway. The peculiar thing was, had it not been for the thud, I would not have noticed I dropped the Bible at all. I had not felt it leave my grasp.

Later, my neurologist told me not to worry about what I had experienced that Sunday. It was fine to continue with my plans to leave for college in a few weeks.

"If it happens again, though, call me."

When I made a last-minute visit to my rheumatologist, he warned me that the college freshman experience might be a source of disillusionment for me.

"I'm ready for anything, sir."

"That is not it," he said. "I know you are excited to be away from home and to meet new friends. You will not have any problem there. I just want to warn you that you may face some inner turmoil when you live in the dorm with all the other girls, that's all."

"Why? I think that dorm life is going to be part of the fun of being in college. I am not worried."

He grew grave. "You have lived with your family until now. Your parents have faced the harsh reality of illness along with you. Nika, some of the girls in the dorm will not understand the depth of your experiences. They are young. Every once in a while, you will come across girls who think breaking up with a boyfriend is the worst thing that could happen. Be patient with them and try not to minimize their feelings. Your health trauma has made you grow up very quickly. I am only suggesting that you find a way to stay eighteen years old in your heart. Allow yourself to be young."

I thought I understood his shadowed warning. Tucking his words in my spiritual suitcase, I raced home to finish packing my physical suitcase.

I enjoyed going off to college even more than I thought I would. Within weeks, I ran for freshman class president, armed with the slogan "Have a Bald with Nika!" It was Becky's idea. She and several of my other friends had enrolled at the same Christian university. We posted political signs all over the campus with great hope in our hearts. Every year since middle school, I had run for class president and lost, with the exception of my freshman year in high school, when I had run uncontested. In college, *many* freshmen candidates ran against me, and I lost yet again. But in the campaign process, "the bald girl" became a recognizable figure among a relatively small student population.

Sure, I met a few girls who were focused on hair spray, like my doctor warned, but most students were looking for a chance to deepen their spiritual relationships with Christ and with one another. I made friends in every class. The professors genuinely cared about more than just academics; they cared about individual students, whom they viewed as vibrant contributors to academia. That time in my life would have been perfect, had I not been quietly tortured by recurrent pain and fatigue. The only viable response was to surrender my health through singing to the Lord, as I always had. A song. Praise in the face of the Wolf. Profound comfort came in a favorite old hymn:

> Take my life and let it be consecrated, Lord, to Thee.
> Take my hands and let them move at the impulse of Thy love,
> At the impulse of Thy love.
> Take my feet and let them be swift and beautiful for Thee.
> Take my voice and let me sing ever, only for my King.
> Ever, only for my King ...

It is not as if praise diminishes present pain, but sometimes it serves as a transcendental instrument, transporting our minds and renewing our strength, refreshing us. As I sang, I was in my own spiritual world, giving a private serenade in the throne room, offering the gift of melody to the Lord. I meant the lyrics. I meant every word.

> *Take my hands.*
> *Take my feet.*
> *Take my voice.*
> *Take my life.*

I knew that if I asked Him to, He would.

TEN

March 1994

BY THE END OF THE WEEK, the ICU waiting room spilled over with visitors; college friends raced to Fort Worth as soon as they heard about our family tragedy. My mother took phone calls from countless others out of town. When she was not stopping in the waiting room to give a report and to greet guests, she sat in a chair at the foot of my bed. There she slept too. If she had eaten a meal since we arrived Wednesday night, I did not know when. She did not leave my side for more than a few minutes at a time.

She was pacing when the doctor walked in. He approached the bed and addressed me directly, as a coherent adult.

"I have a favor to ask of you, dear," he said gently.

My sensation had dulled, and I no longer could distinguish specific textures. But a sliver of hope lay in the fact that at least I *could* feel, however oddly. On my arms and legs, everything felt rough, like sandpaper or tree bark. The doctor touched my forearm with care. His hand seemed to be made of gravel.

"I came here today for a very important reason." Though his voice was tender and measured, he was not communicating with me as if I were a child.

"I am going to a medical conference out of town this weekend. I won't be coming to see you for a few days, but I want you to make me a promise before I go. I am giving you a job to do while I am away," he said, lifting my left hand and placing something on the bed. He rested my palm on top of it.

"When I return on Monday, I am going to come here immediately to see if you kept this stuffed bunny rabbit for me," I could not believe it was a stuffed animal. My senses were completely off kilter, and the plush fabric had felt hard and cold, like a rock. "Your job is to hold on to it until I return. After that, your job will be to keep it. Squeeze my hand if you are willing to make the promise."

Dr. Benton's accent had the quick clip of a New Englander. I had always thought he sounded comforting, even when he spoke with gravity. I trusted him. At that moment, I would have done anything he asked. I tried and tried, but I could not squeeze his hand.

Psychologists tell us that every human being needs to feel needed, that we are sustained by an ongoing sense of purpose. If we do not feel necessary, our psyches simply turn out the lights, and we slide away. That is one reason so many spouses, long married and well into age, follow loved ones in death within months. There is no one left for them to care about intimately, no reason to pour a second cup of coffee, to wait up, to save a seat. There is no one who whispers, "Good morning." There is no one to kiss good night. They mistakenly perceive that there is nothing left for them to do.

For two days on an ICU bed, nothing meaningful had been asked of me. Neither had I something to offer, not a gesture, not a word, not a response of any kind. Though I could not have found the vocabulary to describe my rapid emotional decline at the time, this insightful physician, who cared for the health of the spirit as well as the body, knew. Even a person who is quadriplegic needs something to do.

"She ... she reminds me of my daughter," he said to my mother. "Will you step outside with me for a moment?"

In the hallway, my mother spoke carefully.

"Thank you for bringing her a gift. Your gesture is very sweet, and she will—"

"Mrs. Maples, may I be frank with you?" he interrupted.

My own hearing had become acute. With a loss of sight (only because my eyelids were closed—I could see when the nurses jerked them open), loss of taste (only because nothing had entered my mouth—I could sense the foul taste of bile and stomach-emptiness rising in my throat), and a damaged sense of touch, my senses of hearing and smell intensified. I could tell who was walking into my room by a whiff of perfume or laundry soap, even by the subtle scent of warm skin, before I heard a voice. I could hear conversations from out in the nurses' station as if they were in my own room.

Over the threshold, I listened to the doctor telling my mother that I might have as little as forty-eight hours left to live. *Hours left to live. Hours.* I breathed it in.

Perhaps he wanted me to hear my own prognosis, the

consummate form of respect. A person deserves to know if a measuring tape has been cinched around her days, leaving not "miles to go before I sleep," but only a few precious feet ... or inches.

"We can't be sure," he confessed. "Monday will tell us a lot. If she survives the weekend—*if* she does—we can take an assessment then. Hopefully the speed of her deterioration will not continue."

My mother did not speak.

He made an attempt to explain that, beyond the massive doses of steroids, there was not much more to be done. The damage to my brain stem was extensive. Doctors involved with my case surmised lupus to be attacking my cerebral tissue, the way it had attacked my kidneys years before.

Except you can transplant kidneys, I considered.

"*If* she survives the weekend?" Mother said in a choked voice.

"Now would be a good time to ..." He paused, taking a breath. "If she has one or two special friends who would like to have a moment alone with her, to say good-bye, you should call them now, Mrs. Maples."

Between them the silence swelled.

"Ma'am, if you need—"

"Wait," Mother stopped him, her jaw newly set. "Has anyone ever survived this kind of brain injury?"

"Well ..."

"Has *one* person ever survived?" she said louder.

"Mrs. Maples, if there were some way, some miraculous way, that she could survive a severe episode like this, we don't know that she ever will recover any ability. She may remain in a vegetative state indefinitely. You will have to begin looking into long-term care for her if this is the case, and—"

"I need to know if *one* person has survived and recovered, sir. Please be honest with me." Her voice was a mirror in which my own determination reflected back to me.

My heart rose at the sound of her courage. *This isn't over just yet.*

"Well, yes ... at least *one* person has survived a lupus-induced brain injury of this magnitude."

"That's all I need," she said assuredly, turning to walk away. Case closed.

"Mrs. Maples, I need to tell you," he warned, "her survival was day to day, but now it is second to second."

Becky came first. She scraped a chair across the hard floor and sat down beside the bed.

"Nika ...," she started and then stopped, taking my hand. I could feel one of her tears running down my desensitized arm like a thin scratch. "They told me that I could come in here to be with you ..." She swallowed hard on her sorrow.

A nurse came in to check vital signs, so Becky pulled back and waited a few minutes before continuing when we were alone.

"They also told me not to mention anything sad ... only to talk to you like I usually would ... but I ..."

There was a long silence. Breathing soundly, she waited. Then she began again with strength.

"Nika, I ache because I know that you are aching. Our lifelong memories flood my heart, and the last thing I want to think about is you going away now. But there is something I want you to know. You can go. You can go, if you need to.

I am going to see you again in Heaven one day. We all will; I'm *sure* of it. I don't want you to leave us, but if you need to ... you can go."

She fumbled for words, jarred by the sound next to her: my heart monitor kept time, the very time that was ticking away from us.

Her voice held her heart now. "I feel like I am losing my right arm today." She inhaled deeply.

"If I lose you, I will have to learn how to do things again, left-handed. I can do it, but ... Nika, I will never forget how it felt to have a right arm."

She began to tell several of her fondest recollections aloud and only stopped when she started to cry. My greatest pain was my inability to voice a shared grief. I was losing her too. Our unspoken, unshakable faith sustained us through our silence. By the time she left the room, I felt peaceful, comforted.

Another dear friend, Cole, cried too, but his tears seemed different. When he walked into the room, I recognized his bracing outdoor scent. He did not speak, but I sensed he stood close. He waited for a long time, studying me. Then he sat down, pulled my weak hand into both of his, and wept. He leaned over my still body, and his tears soaked through the thin hospital gown, rolling down my rib cage to the bed.

His sobs resonated through me. He was in a cave of despair, the kind of echoing ache created by a lack of belief. As long as I had known him, he had struggled to have faith. God was not real to him. So Cole's head spun in the dizzying reality of an intensive care unit, and he had nothing to lean on, to grab for support.

If Jesus is just a man to us, our anguish means nothing. Life is empty. We are empty.

Therefore, we must choose to cultivate belief, to bring in a mighty harvest, during our living moments—the fertile season when we seem to need it the least. For in the drought of our dying days, faith will be our food. And we will be full.

Although Becky had grieved, she grieved with the promise of Providence. But Cole's tears fell hopelessly, as if they were splashing on the lid of a coffin, not on a breathing body. I could almost feel the difference. Becky had assured me that we would experience a joyous reunion eventually, even if it would be after this life on earth. I could tell that Cole was not so convinced. Juxtaposed, the two farewells left completely different tastes in my motionless mouth.

God is Earth's only hope.

"Good-bye," Cole whispered, meaning forever. He rose from his chair after some time. When he left, I felt stunned, shaken.

Then I was in the cave alone.

I could not help thinking that Becky and Cole had just given my eulogy. In all my life, I had never imagined I would be within earshot.

Around eleven o'clock that night, my father lay on a sleeping bag on the floor. The last nurse turned off the buzzing overhead light. I heard him rustle the nylon to get settled, and soon he was snoring.

My mother shifted, trying to find respite in her awkward vinyl chair. She propped both ankles on the corner of the bed, forcing the blanket down tight on my feet. She did not know this was painful for me; she was in discomfort herself. Two days of attending to me for hours had caused her feet to swell and throb. A nurse had given her a tiny lamp that gynecologists use for examinations, and by its light, she began her daily crossword puzzle. I could hear her fold the newspaper into a handy, workable size. It was the same thin sound I had heard all my life but had not noticed until that moment.

Some time later, I fell into a deep sleep.

At 3:00 AM, my father abruptly sat up. He rushed to my side so quickly the movement jostled me into awareness.

"What's wrong?" he said aloud, panting. The room was silent, save the vigilant medical equipment, which told him that my heart rate was twenty-four beats per minute. It had stayed around 30 bpm since I had been in the ICU.

He placed his hand on my chest and throat. He opened my mouth. He moved my hand so that he could study the IV site. He repositioned the oxygen tube and checked the heart and oxygen sensors. He walked around the bed, squeezing my legs and arms lightly.

"What's wrong?" he whispered to himself, leaning on the bed rail.

I recorded information in miniscule bits: The lights were off. The ICU was still. Nurses at the station were speaking softly. It must be very late. I did not hear my mother stir. The pressure of her feet was gone from the bed. I could not smell her. She must have moved while I was asleep. The heart monitor blipped, but it seemed to be slowing. Suddenly I felt so weak.

Am I still alive?

Then my father pulled back my eyelids, and the room shook when he yelled.

ELEVEN

IMAGINE THE LONE SECRETARY squirting grocery-label grape juice from the plastic pipette of a turkey baster, or from a squeeze bottle with its no-drip spout, into miniature, disposable Communion cups, just like any loyal secretary in any small rural church anywhere. See the team of deacons dispensing a similarly measured sip from the sanitary and ultrafast patented juice dispenser, with its plurality of tubes and precise mechanism, into a squadron of waiting cups, just like any devoted deacons in any urban megachurch anywhere.

Though this tidy idea of communing with Christ is conducted this way out of necessity, I am always taken by the mirth of it. Our contemporary practice—so sweet, so neat—does not hint at the intoxication that a committed, abiding relationship with Him entails. His blood dizzies us. The chalice is as dangerous as a shot glass. The more of Him we imbibe, the more we want—the more we want, the more we need just to make it through the day.

In Mark 10, the Lord asked the sons of Zebedee, "Can you drink from the cup I drink?"

"We can," they answered.

Jesus said to them, "You will."

By now we all know they did not understand how badly the swallow would burn. Jesus knew. He knew the power in the Blood, the sting in it, the fire. He knew that it would go down less like diluted fruit juice and more like Kentucky Straight Bourbon, which we need before He cuts into us.

We are asking God to pull the "evil stuff" out, are we not? We are crying for Him to extract the inner sin that hobbles our hearts. Of course, there will be pain in the process. When God prunes our spirits, it is not pretty. Only a lunatic would lie down and invite such a brute operation. Only a man who is drunk on the Fruit of the very Vine he loves. When we enter into Communion, then, let us metaphorically take the swig of this holy wine before we bite the bullet, as if we are silver-screen cowboys gulping from a jug just before He draws arrowhead fragments and snake venom from our trembling limbs.

God stands at the ready to take from us our peril. He doesn't hesitate. In Isaiah 51:22, we read the Lord's intent, "See, I have taken out of your hand the cup that made you stagger; from that cup, the goblet of my wrath, you will never drink again."

Oh, praise the Lord for His taking.

And praise the Lord that we drink from a new cup.

Shortly after I began my collegiate studies, God whispered that I should take a sip because He was preparing to prune. In my heart, Self-Reliance had grown tall, spreading dangerous seeds on the wind: Bitterness, Silent-Suffering, Jealousy. My thoughts had become knotty with weeds. The Gardener wanted me to participate with Him in the backbreaking work of spiritual agriculture, to get my hands dirty, to yank the suffocating overgrowth out. Most garden weeds are not detrimental in and of themselves. Many look lovely. Their harm comes in the way they grow where they do not belong, creating conditions in which the development of intentional plants cannot occur. They sap the soil of nourishment; they crowd out sunlight. They stop the good from growing. God had already planted a lot of beneficial seedlings in my soul. Still, He wanted me to root out the nuisances that were preventing the maturation of His beautiful blooms. He wanted me to spend more time seeking His description of the "good works He had prepared in advance" (Ephesians 2:10) for me to do. He wanted me to let go of the perceived safety of my own plan. He wanted me to cooperate, to kneel beside Him in the garden, but I did not.

When I would not listen to the gentle hum of His heartbeat, when I would not keep my ear close to His chest, when I would not stay beside the quiet waters, He loved me enough to lay me down. And what could have been cooperation turned into an operation. There was not enough time to bite any bullet before the incision began. The process would be nothing less than coronary bypass surgery. The Great Physician had to cut the illusions out of my heart. And He certainly "bypassed" my permission to do so. Lovingly, He would teach me that I must not pretend to rely on myself any longer. My pruning began at a time when I thought my worst health problems were coming to an end. They were only beginning.

I had an early morning chemo treatment at the beginning of the three-week Christmas vacation my freshman year in college, and I was determined that nothing would ruin my days at home. During the treatment, however, they forgot to add the antinausea medication to the intravenous drip. The oncologist prescribed an oral alternative, Compazine, and told me to take one pill *every six hours*. I drove straight to the pharmacy and popped one before I even left the parking lot.

Five hours posttreatment, I usually started vomiting profusely, even when the antinausea supplement was in the drip, but with the Compazine pills, I felt fine. In fact, I felt well enough to call several friends. We made plans to play outdoor miniature golf that evening; such is winter in Texas. It was the first time I ever felt strong enough to be social on a chemo day. I hung up the phone and took another Compazine pill. *Just in case*, I told myself.

Three hours later, I felt mildly nauseated, so I took another one.

My friends were scheduled to gather at my house at 7:00 PM. An hour before they came, I started feeling dizzy. I had to lie down on the couch, just to keep from falling over. Strangely, I felt my eyes pulling upward and to the right. With concentration, I could force myself to look straight ahead, but the effort made me dizzier, so I closed my eyes.

"I really wish you would stay at home and get some rest, Nika. I don't think it is a good idea to go out with your friends tonight," my mother requested, sitting next to me on the couch.

I rested my forearm on my eyelids and did not look at her. "It's just the chemo. This always happens. Don't worry about it; I'll take a Compazine."

"Haven't you already taken one today?"

"Don't worry about it, Mother," I growled. She left to meet a friend at the movies. When I heard her lock the front door behind her, I pulled myself together and struggled to the bathroom, where I forced down another Compazine. Then I lay back on the couch and waited for my friends to arrive. I fell asleep.

When the doorbell rang, the noise startled me awake. I lay there. It rang again. I was just too weak to get up to answer the door. My friends rang again. I tried to ease off the couch so that I could crawl to the front door, a few feet away. I could move a little, but not with enough power to roll my body to the floor. They rang the bell again. I could hear them talking outside for a long time.

"Why isn't she coming to the door?" one questioned. He rang again and pounded his fist hard.

"Maybe she is at Becky's house. Let's go see," the other offered. Becky's family lived across the street.

"You can go check. I'll stay. I think she is in here. Maybe she's hurt." Then they shouted to me, "Nika! Nika, if you are in there, you had better say so, because we are about to break down this door!"

They continued knocking, shouting, and ringing the bell. I was close enough that if I had yelled, the boys would have heard me, but my jaw had locked shut. My teeth started grinding, and I was choking on my tongue. I made a guttural sound as loudly as I could. My eyes pulled forcefully upward now.

Suddenly they heaved their shoulders into the door as if it were a football blocking sled. The catch gave way, and they fell inside. Both boys ran to me.

"What's wrong? Tell us what's wrong!"

Only my frenzied eyes fired an answer. I could not speak.

The rest of our friends arrived moments later. The loss of strength and sudden inability to control my body felt like a spell. Instantly and without explanation, the spell broke, and I could speak and move. The boys were stunned. They looked at me and at each other in disbelief as I got up off the couch, wiping my mouth and working my fists, open and closed, open and closed. I greeted my entering friends and asked them to wait a few minutes while I freshened up. Sweat had soaked my clothes.

In my mother's bathroom, I ran the tap and got a washcloth. I looked at myself in the mirror.

What just happened to me?

Standing there, I took a few deep breaths. Abruptly, I felt my eyes rotating upward and to the far right, like they were being pulled by invisible strings. I could hardly see.

Ten minutes later, they found me lying on my mother's bed. My head was craning so far to the right it looked like my neck would snap. Petrified, my friends saw my hands curling, pinned to my chest with fingers drawn inward toward my palms like claws. With teeth grinding, my jaw locked again. I could not speak.

Immediately, they set to work with valiance, wasting no time. Becky sat on the bed with me and pulled my hand softly into hers. She started to pray aloud. "Lord, we don't know what is happening, but *You* do ..."

The others ran around the house, trying to find clues to my mother's whereabouts. This was long before we all had cell phones. Someone found a note on the kitchen counter, listing movie locations and times. There was a shout of discovery.

A friend scooped me off the bed and carried me to the car. Becky drove us to the emergency room.

"Lord, help us know what to do, where to go ..." She was still praying.

Two went to hunt for my mother. They bet on one of the movie theaters, then picked one of the movies on the cryptic kitchen list. Miraculously, they found her on the first try. I can only imagine what she felt when they crept through the darkened movie theater and whispered down her row, "Something's wrong with Nika! We've taken her to the emergency room!"

The first speeding carload arrived at the hospital. They found a wheelchair and pushed me up to the receptionist's counter, panting and panicked. I was coiled like a spastic spring in the chair.

"Is she taking any medication?" the receptionist asked, seeming somewhat bored by the uneventful evening.

"Chemotherapy!" everyone said in unison.

"Uh-huh. We'll be with you in a moment." The receptionist calmly walked away from her desk. A few quiet patients sat in the waiting room.

I began throwing up. My jaw was still locked. With all my strength, I tried to force my mouth to open. Seconds later I could not hold my jaw apart, and it snapped shut on my tongue. The metallic tang of blood filled my mouth.

A nurse walked out of the double doors and took the handles of the wheelchair from my friends, "We've got it from here." When he turned, the doors swung behind him, abruptly cutting off any followers.

My stomach had stopped heaving, but my head still craned to the right in a painful torque. Nurses stripped my wet, nasty clothes and lay me down on the bed. They covered me with a sheet and left me alone, shivering in fear.

A few minutes later, the doctor sat down on the side of the bed. He sighed loudly. "Your friends tell me you are taking chemotherapy, right?"

I tried to nod, wincing from the pain in my neck.

"Are you taking antinausea drugs along with that?"

A nod.

"Like Compazine?" He sounded irritated.

Another agonizing nod.

He stood to go. Before he left, he spoke quietly to a nurse, who hurried away and came back with a syringe.

"This is Benadryl," she said. "Be still while I stick you a little bit."

That was all it took. My muscles relaxed and my eyes returned to a forward gaze within minutes. I was so relieved I started to cry. The doctor returned to my bedside with my mother.

"Nika, did you even bother to read your medicine bottle?" he said.

Though I could speak again, I avoided his gaze and only nodded. My neck was sore.

"How often were you supposed to take this drug?" he asked pointedly.

"Every six hours."

"And how often *did* you take it?"

I lifted my face to him. "Too often, sir."

He looked at my mother in a communicative way and then back at me. "You learned your lesson the hard way. Prescription instructions are there for a reason. You were very lucky on this one, young lady. Very lucky."

By the second semester, my hair was full and soft, brand-new. Before it fell out, it had been thin, stringy, and a light honey shade of brown. I was not that sorry to be rid of it and had been hoping that my second head of hair would bring the curls that are some chemo patients' reward. Instead, my new hair grew in straight, but it amused me to note that it was thicker and darker, a mahogany brown. Like my wig.

Though I still continued to receive monthly doses of chemo, my hair never thinned again. Doctors suggested that the first overwhelming blast of chemo had caused the initial damage, and all other doses were not intense enough to sustain hair loss. General weakness, vomiting, fatigue, and mouth and nose lesions continued. In addition to chemotherapy, I took Prednisone. My physician had prescribed a daily dose at the same time that I began Cytoxan chemotherapy two years before. Severe arthritic pain plagued me every day, and no other medication brought relief like the steroids. As long as I stayed above 10 mg, the pain was bearable. As long as I stayed below 20 mg, my face did not swell, so I did not complain. Together, the Cytoxan and Prednisone brought my blood work and general sense of wellness back into a reasonable range. Talk of an urgent surgical response faded. Both kidneys appeared stable, and for the most part, I felt like I was bouncing back, albeit slowly and uncomfortably.

Joint aches followed me into June. I limped when my ankles hurt and winced when my fingers swelled, but I had long since learned to disguise both chemo side effects and lupus pain. A person with a chronic illness enters a homeostasis of silence, knowing that most friends tire of hearing about constant discomfort, and over time, some friends even start to doubt its existence. There was no time to linger in despair or complaint, anyway; bolstering my summer schedule became a priority. At home in the Dallas/Fort Worth Metroplex, I applied for temporary jobs at local restaurants, but they had met their unwritten quota of college kids on vacation. When someone recommended that I look into several summer job openings at DFW airport, I applied there too. On the spot, an airport service company hired me to push passengers who use wheelchairs around one of the four terminals. I wore a uniform: a light blue shirt with gold patches on the sleeves, a little navy necktie, and navy slacks. I looked like a street busker's monkey.

There was not as much wheelchair-pushing to be done as we "pushes" would have liked. Mostly we sat in small pockets, a few gates between each group, throughout the terminal. A group consisted of five pushes and one coordinator, who waited for the dispatcher's voice to crackle over the walkie-talkie: "Push to Gate 10. Push to Gate 10." The group stationed closest to Gate 10 would come to life for the moment.

"This is Kevin's call. The rest of y'all just sit back down."

We rotated the calls, and on your turn to push, you crossed your fingers and hoped for a wealthy wheelchair user. At worst, the traveler will be a ponderous grandfather coming from San Antonio to visit his grandchildren in Fort Worth, and then you might groan inwardly, both because the Jetway ramp is steep enough to cause a hernia if the passenger is heavy *and* because there will not be a tip, even though waiting for baggage and loading the car will make you miss your next turn for a push. At best, the traveler will be an aging socialite on her way from her estate in Beverly Hills to meet some Dallas acquaintances before heading on to a European destination, and then you might wink at your fellow pushes as she relaxes in the chair, not because she will be a light passenger (her massive Louis Vuitton carry-on makes up the difference), but because the tip will be at least thirty dollars. If the connecting flight is several gates away, it might be as much as fifty.

As the pushes waited for long minutes at a time for the next dispatch, we played in the wheelchairs that we had checked out from the office for the day. There were some favorite chairs that made for an extra-smooth ride and some lemons that had quirky wheels. The pushes who arrived earliest would snatch up the good chairs before they even clocked in for the day. Then the waiting activities began. We would sit in the chairs ourselves, wheeling back and forth, back and forth, turning tight corners, parallel parking, popping wheelies (which I never mastered), and racing one another in the dawn hours when certain parts of the terminal were not yet teeming with people.

I became quite adept at working with a wheelchair, both pushing myself and pushing others. When my sophomore year started, I would have said that the only thing I got out of my two months as a wheelchair push was a little bit of pocket change, new friends I probably never would see again, and some irrelevant finesse in basic wheelchair operation. Only a short time later, it would become more relevant than I could have imagined.

That fall I took eighteen hours of coursework, declaring broadcast journalism as my major. Through my mass communication courses, I worked a few hours a week as an announcer at a campus radio station, which had been created as a laboratory for budding broadcasters. Activity and joy rang through every sunlit moment; I studied quietly at night.

"Finally, this is how college life is supposed to be," I would say to myself, sighing, as I typed papers and read textbooks into the early morning hours.

Somehow, I pulled it off. Without dropping any extracurricular activity, I enrolled in another eighteen hours that January and started envisioning life without Cytoxan. All the chemical misery would be over in April. I just needed to hang on a few more months. My mind offered this rational comfort during my worst moments.

As I slept, a dream convinced me that I might not have that much time.

I am in a room without light. Everywhere I turn, there is darkness.

A small flame dances to life, and its faint glow illuminates the space. I can barely see the table in front of me. On the table is a birthday cake, frosted thickly in pink. Ribbons of white icing drape around the crest of the cake. On top, something is written in white, but from where I am seated, I cannot read the words. I think it may be my name. The flame radiates from one white candle in the center of the cake. It flickers quickly as if there is breath or an open window nearby. Beyond the cake, the room is black; I cannot see the edges of the table.

For some time, I stare at the cake and the candle. Now I am sure the cake is for me. A voice, a whisper, touches my face in a rush of air. I realize someone is sitting in the room with me, across the table. He is darkly shadowed.

I listen to his breath, paralyzed by terror.

Slowly he speaks, stirring the flame, "You will not turn

twenty-one."

Then he blows out the candle, and there is nothing but darkness.

When I opened my eyes, I could not catch my breath for several minutes. My hand clutched my chest weakly. I was alone in the dorm room. Struggling to the bathroom to splash water on my face, I leaned on the sink and looked in the mirror.

That wasn't a dream.

I shuddered for the first of many times throughout that day. Making my way from class to class, I told no one about what I had seen in the night. I just smiled. I had to; it was my twentieth birthday.

At dusk, I dumped out my jar of tips from the Italian restaurant where I waited tables and went to the mall.

Growing up amid financial tumult meant that my athletic shoes always had been pleather and had come from some major discount store. Mom had a thing about never wearing clothes or shoes with a visible brand or logo.

"You and God define who you are, that's it," she said. "Your name and His are the only names that should go before you. Even if we had enough money for these things, you are never so small a person that you should walk around, serving as a billboard to advertise somebody else's company or name. You matter in your own right. You have a mouth; you speak for yourself. Don't let your clothes speak louder."

Of course this opinion made me furious in middle school, when I wanted to mask my insecurity with a logo that had the popular crowd's approval. As I grew into young adulthood, my mother's wisdom unveiled itself. She was teaching me not to need outward endorsement in order to feel worthy of attention. When I finally understood its significance, I fully adopted her philosophy where clothes with visible brands are concerned, but on my twentieth birthday, I wanted to splurge on some nice running shoes, for once, to buy quality athletic shoes that might have an obvious logo.

Shopping for those shoes was such a pleasure. I took my time walking around the mall by myself, enjoying every window display. After the long and delicate dance of deliberation with which a child chooses a special candy, I finally selected a white pair with purple and neon pink accents. I am sure I walked out of the store with a goofy smile on my face.

The next day, I woke up before daylight to run. I do not remember anything about the route that morning. I do not remember if it was a mild Texas winter or bitterly cold, if I ran alone or if there were other students jogging around the campus. I do not remember if it was cloudy or clear, if the planter boxes bloomed or still suffered from an icy chill. I do not remember if I returned to my room in time to relax and linger over breakfast, or if I showered and dressed in a hurry.

I might have paid attention to the aesthetic details of my first run in those shoes, had I known that it would also be my last.

12

THE HEADACHE CHIPPED INTO MY SKULL like an ice pick. Unlike any other headache I had experienced, this was not a dull, general, or radiating sensation. It did not throb. The pain drilled like a singular beam of pressure an inch or two behind my left temple. No pain reliever even softened the edge. I could cover the small spot with my thumb, and sometimes I would press into it, hoping for a minor ease in the tension when I pulled away. The spike never relented.

When the headache stopped a few days later, I did not notice. By then the pain that gnawed at my arthritic limbs distracted me. All joints felt porous, brittle. At work I lifted heavy trays of lasagna and spaghetti with a grimace, the way a weight lifter leverages a competitive barbell. It became too much for my wrists.

One evening when I was serving a large party of five young families from a nearby Air Force base, I could not balance the tray of thick cocktail schooners. As I was leaning over to place a mug of beer on the table with my right hand, my left arm started to shake. My wrist felt like it was breaking under the weight of the tray. Before I could catch it, the tray of drinks dumped onto the table. A heavy blue frozen margarita toppled directly onto one of the mothers. She was holding an infant. To my horror, the icy mixture slid down her shoulder and onto the baby. Instantly, everyone pushed away from the table, and the women screamed, dabbing their dresses with fabric napkins. I tried to help the woman with the baby, but her husband motioned for me to leave her alone. The restaurant manager moved the party to a clean section, dismissing their bill and assigning their table to another member of the waitstaff.

"Just go home, Nika," he said gruffly, raking fingers through his tousled hair. Later, he would take their entire bill out of my paycheck.

In the restaurant bathroom, I ripped off my apron and barely made it into a stall before I started vomiting. As soon as I could stop, I slipped through the dining areas and out into the parking lot.

The restaurant was only twenty minutes from my dormitory. I needed to get home to rest. Rubbing my swollen wrist, I inhaled the brisk January night air to clear my head. I had to admit something was desperately wrong. Inside my car, I rested my forehead on the chilly steering wheel, and I prayed for the young servicemen and women whose evening I had just ruined. Then I prayed for myself.

"Lord, what is happening to me? Please let me get some rest tonight. I just want to sleep."

Dealing with chemotherapy had become such a way of life over the past two years that I always was prepared. I had a few paper grocery bags for this purpose in the glove compartment and had to use one as I drove back to campus. By the time I got to my dorm room, my pain had intensified. I could hardly move. I tried to unbutton my shirt, but the process was excruciating. I gave up and decided to sleep in my clothes, grunting as I pried off my shoes. I did not wake up until almost evening the next day, having slept straight through my alarm and an entire day's worth of classes. I had never slept that long at one time. Friends had been calling and calling. There were over fifteen messages blinking on the machine, but I had never heard the phone ring. Even after sleeping close to twenty hours, I did not feel rested; the pain and fatigue remained the same. When I put on clothes and some makeup to go to the cafeteria, I looked intently in the mirror. On top of my left cheek, near my nose, there was a thin blister I had never seen before. I touched it and jumped back from the sting. I had never experienced a lupus butterfly rash before, and I did not know if this was how they began.

Please, God, no.

Ambling through a cafeteria dinner in solitude, I returned to my dorm room and went back to sleep.

A couple of weeks later, I pulled out of the restaurant parking lot after my shift, late on a Monday night. I drove in the cold, biting rain. After about ten minutes, a dark curtain pulled over the vision in my left eye. It started slowly; I thought something was outside the driver's side window. But the darkness continued from the corner nearest my temple toward my nose. Still driving, I waved a hand in front of my face and groped for my eyelid.

Is it open?

My left eye was blind.

I punched the gas pedal and sped toward the dorm. Like my mother, I am calm in a crisis. There was no panic. There were only questions to be answered.

Will this happen to my right eye? Am I going blind? How much time do I have? Should I pull over or try to make it to the dorm so that I can call someone? Would it be dangerous to pull over in this part of town late at night?

No, I have to speed home. I am halfway there.

I crashed through my dorm door and ran to the phone. My mother picked up, but even as I described what happened, my vision started to return. I told her about the awful joint pain and the headache.

"You usually know when you should go to the emergency room. Is this one of those times? There is only so much I can do for you from two hundred miles away. Let's decide the next step together."

I told her that I would just go to bed. It *was* one of those times when I felt I needed medical attention and needed it immediately. But I also knew that doctors rarely had a definitive answer where my lupus was concerned. They would just wait to see the next development of the mysterious disease. At times I felt like a living experiment. I was accustomed to sleeping overnight in a hospital, only to be sent home the next day with no solutions.

We hung up and she vowed to call the doctor first thing in the morning. That night the pain racked my body. I did not cry into the pillow. I screamed.

I quit my job at the restaurant the next morning before heading to Fort Worth for the doctor's appointment my mother had arranged. It was February 14. I asked a friend to drive me, because I had continued to lose vision in my left eye for fifteen minutes at a time on three more occasions that morning. She tried to keep my girlish spirits up; it *was* Valentine's Day, after all. We giggled as we drove, joking that we were heading to the kind of "date" I would never forget.

"This could be a romantic Valentine's Day after all; you never know," she said. "Maybe the doctor will be young and handsome."

"Um ... nice try. I already know the doctor," I said, shaking my head definitively.

"So maybe the nurse will be male, then," she suggested, smiling.

"I guess I could flirt with the phlebotomist," I chortled, trying to be lighthearted, avoiding the dreadful intuition in my gut. Turning to the window, I watched miles of mesquite stretch into a blur.

Though the MRI of my brain revealed nothing unusual, my physician was more than a little concerned. He was emphatic, begging me to stay home for a few days to rest. But because of the physical strain that had been occurring over the last few weeks, I had skipped one of my classes so many times that I was denied credit. I did not want to jeopardize the rest of my academic load, because I had reached the maximum absences for those courses too. I decided not to stay home.

We drove back to the university the same evening. There was not as much levity on the return trip. I am not sure why I brought the MRI films along with me, but I found myself staring at the silhouette of my skull as we drove. It was uncomfortable to speculate about my condition, so we were silent for the better part of the two-and-a-half-hour ride.

Episodic blindness plagued my left eye for another week. It

never lasted longer than thirty minutes at a time. That weekend, Mother came to my campus to watch me perform with my sorority in a campuswide variety show. It was in my dorm room late that Friday night when I told her about my right arm.

"It feels like it is on fire, Mom." I reached up and indicated the area between my elbow and armpit, on the soft underside of my right bicep. "Just there. Can you see anything? The sensation is so strange." She lightly ran her index finger over the area. I recoiled.

"Ouch! I told you it hurt!" I said sharply, pulling away. "I just don't get it," I said, bowing my head in frustration. "Even when the fabric from my shirt touches that spot, I have to try hard to concentrate; it is really painful."

"This worries me," she said. "Is there anything else I should know?"

"Well ..." After a moment, I sat down on the bed and rolled up the right cuff of my jeans. "There is this one spot on my leg where ... I ..." Pausing, I searched for a way to pull the words from my throat.

"What is it, Nika?" she whispered, reaching out to touch my shinbone carefully. This time I did not jerk away.

"I ... can't feel anything."

THIRTEEN

March 1994

TWO ICU NURSES CAME RUNNING when they heard my father's cry. He demanded that they call the night resident at once.

When he had opened my lids, both eyes had fallen to face opposite walls. I was awake and eager to see the room, without the blinding glare of a nurse's penlight shining in my pupils. But I could not make sense of what I saw. Without contacts or glasses, I am visually impaired, yet I can make out general shapes and colors. This time I could not. I was seeing both sides of the room at the same time, but not in a focused, cohesive way. My eyes were no longer working in tandem. They bounced and wiggled in the far corners of my eye sockets.

My brain stem, suddenly swelling and herniating, was crushing my ocular nerve.

"I said, call the resident!" my father ordered the nurses for the third time.

"We already called for her. She's asleep on another floor."

"Get her anyway!"

The hurricane of ire flung around the room by my father should have been enough to wake the young physician where she lay in her recliner upstairs. Nurses ran to get her, and she came. My father jerked back my eyelids to show her.

"Do you see *this*? And you were *not* going to come down here!"

The resident leaned over to look. Then she turned to him, her own face blank.

"Do you need me to tell you what to do? Call the neurologist!" he said.

She shrugged. "What do I tell him?"

"Call him *now*!" he exploded.

She hurriedly walked out of the room, and when she returned a few minutes later, she reported, "The doctor said he would be here for rounds at nine."

"By nine he might as well order a coroner's report!" my father shouted, stomping back to my bedside, where the resident began examining my feet and ankles. I could tell she was wearing long, artificial nails; their sharpness dug into my soles. She handled me roughly, as if I were not really there. My father paced and snorted, gruff as a grizzly bear.

I could not tell what was happening; I wanted someone to explain.

What is wrong with my eyes? What is all this about?

Across town, the neurologist tried to go back to sleep, but could not. Something nagged at his thoughts. He gave up, deciding to dress to come to the hospital. He arrived close to 3:30 AM. After one look at my eyes, he snapped an order for medication that would reduce the swelling on the inside of my skull. All anyone could do was pray.

There are many conduits of communication. The longer I was away from the use of the outer conduits of mouth, eye, and hand, the more I inclined toward the inner conduits of heart, mind, and soul. I was not as imprisoned as it may have seemed. The outward man, as soon as he was restrained, released the inward man to activity. Once my body was motionless, my spirit began to move.

"Peace! Be still!" The Lord had spoken into my storm. And I was completely still. For the first time, I was at peace and I could hear Him clearly. I could hear and, within my mind, I could *see*.

I am on the rim of a desert gorge. No green thing grows within my view. The trough of the ravine is burdened with boulders, sharp passageways any foot traveler would curse. In a tightening circle, high above the jagged cliffs, vultures cry out. This is the *Valley of the Shadow of Death*.

"You must cross now," a Voice says, warmly.

"I'm afraid."

"I will walk with you," He offers.

I turn to see a familiar hand, extending to me. I take hold of it and am reassured. I have no more questions. I have no more questions. I have no more questions. Everything that mattered to me before does not matter anymore. There is nothing but our Father's love, abiding as it always has. Any "Topics for Heaven," anything I might have listed, disintegrates. I HAVE NO MORE QUESTIONS.

He is the Answer.

We walk through shrieking rocks and ashen bones. All the while, He is holding my hand. I am safe.

Another Voice, both above and around us, speaks, "For I consider that our present sufferings are not worth comparing with the glory that will be revealed in us."

We walk for many hazardous miles. The Voice with us keeps repeating, "For I consider that our present sufferings are not worth comparing with the glory ..."

I am content to be here, though the terrain is treacherous. The Answer is the Father.

We climb the towering edge of the opposite side, and He lets go. I still have not seen anything but His strong hand.

"You must go back."

I think He means that I must go back through Death's Valley, and I turn to climb down into it.

"I am ready." Suddenly, I only want to walk with Him, no matter where we go.

"No. You must go back." Now I know He wants me to walk back into Life, and I scream out, unwilling to leave His side.

"I can't!" My cry spills throughout the canyon.

"Write what you have seen," He says.

"Write! How can I? I can't move!"

"I will not hinder My message."

I fall to my knees and bury my face in my hands, pressing my forehead hard in the dirt. I am shaking with tears.

When I look up, He is rising away—not floating ethereally, not flying with great movement, but simply traveling vertically as we would travel horizontally. He can move this way. Now He is looking down on me, arms open as if I should come to Him.

He is indicating that I can still come to Him. The Answer is Jesus.

I do not want to face this thing. I do not want to go back.

Again, the quiet Voice around me breathes, "For I consider that our present sufferings are not worth comparing with the glory that will be revealed in us." The Answer is the Spirit.

I have no more questions.

My tears make mud of the dust.

When I awoke, it was Saturday morning; I could sense gray sunlight coming through the only window. The heart monitor kept time, though the rest of the room was still. My mother lightly snored in her chair. A nurse walked in and quietly pulled back the blanket and swept aside my gown to administer my morning Heparin shot.

I do not want to be here.

I started thinking of ways to die.

14 FOURTEEN

MY MOTHER ONLY AGREED to leave town when I shook the MRI films in a fury.

"Do you see *these*?" I shouted at her. "The doctors did not know anything on Valentine's Day, and they will not know anything now! I am not going to the doctor, and that's the last word on the subject!"

Tension had been building between us for some time. The stress of single motherhood was sapping her of strength, because her job paid just enough to cover the basics. Dad's financial help was erratic, at best. A few times, Mom had to ask for the canned goods that the community center could not serve to needy families because they were dented and damaged. She was willing to take them. Our church also helped pay the utility bills. Once, a Good Samaritan left a few necessities in a grocery bag on our porch.

When the friend who had been allowing our family to live, rent-free, in his house needed it for another purpose, Dad came through unexpectedly. He signed a contract on a brand-new home for us. In her financial shape, my mother could not have signed a contract on a doghouse.

She and Mark, my brother, had moved into a rental property during construction, a stopgap measure that was less than ideal. When she discovered that rats were living there with them, eating from medicine bottles and boxes of pancake mix and nesting with bits of cardboard and pillow stuffing, she could not wait to move out. I had packed my room but did not want to leave the university for another weekend to help her do anything else. It was a lot easier to avoid thoughts about my father's absence and the devastation that remained, which continued to wreck my heart. Every time I would think about it more than superficially, I would lose my appetite and would not eat or sleep for a few days.

Avoidance was the wrong avenue of escape. Equally erroneous was blaming my mother for our broken family, which I often did. She was hurt and angered by this accusation, so we fought over both significant and meaningless things.

When she stormed out of my dorm room that weekend, we muttered good-byes, but not with pleasant expressions on our faces. She was headed to a living room full of moving boxes, none of which had been unpacked and some of which had served as public transportation for rodent roommates. She had heard them scratching. One had scampered boldly through the new dining room as if Mom and Mark were living in *his* new house.

I was facing another week of trying to lug myself through the scholastic mire I had created by skipping so much class.

But on Monday, I was too woozy to go to any class. I stayed

in bed with the bedspread pulled over my face like a corpse. The only thing I could do was to stagger to the bathroom or to the desk drawer for a granola bar. After sleeping all day, I called Mother and told her I was coming back to Fort Worth the next morning. She said she would arrange for a spur-of-the-moment doctor's appointment.

Because I was still going blind sporadically, a couple of friends drove, dropping me off on the porch of the new house. I had never been inside and did not have a key, so I waited until my mother got home from work a short time later.

Her tires squealed into the driveway.

"The doctor wants us to go straight to the hospital for tests," she said. She opened the van door, starting to explain before she turned off the engine and stepped out.

"No! I am not going into the hospital!" I yelled. "I thought I was coming for an office appointment, that's all."

"Things changed. I told him that you were dizzy last night and had trouble walking. I told him you kept falling over when you tried to get your keys out of your purse or climbed the stairs. When he heard that you could not do two simple things at once because you were so disoriented, he told me to get you to the hospital the moment you came into town."

"No, Mom ..."

She narrowed her eyes at me. They were pewter in the winter sunlight.

"Please do not start this," she pleaded. "Nika, he is very concerned. I could hear it in his voice. This time is different. This time is different."

But it was no different. An MRI, a CT scan, and a spinal

tap later, there was still no conclusive evidence concerning my condition. The test that had been most difficult to undergo was the angiogram. In the operating room, a neurologist had made a small incision in my groin and inserted a tube that ran from the top of my thigh all the way to the base of my skull. They needed me to be conscious and completely still during the test. It took a long time, and I was terrified. I could not stop shaking, even after they administered light sedation. The neurologist told the nurses that my movement was dangerous, and he ordered another dose. I felt the second wave and was calmer. Then the doctor injected iodine into the tube at the site of the incision. A second later, I tasted metal on my tongue, and a small area inside the base of my skull began to burn. Never before or since have I felt—actually been fully aware of—the mass of my cerebral tissue. I could feel my brain. The trembling began again, this time more violently. The neurologist ordered a third dose of sedative, and I was out.

I woke up in my hospital room and muttered some slurred question to my mother.

"You are groggy. Here, take a drink and then go back to sleep, Nika." She tilted a cup to give me a sip of water and then stood over the bed until I closed my eyes and slept.

Several hours later, I stirred. The lights in the room were off, and my mother napped in a reclining chair nearby.

"Mudder," I groaned. She sat up and bolted to my side.

"What is it? How are you feeling?"

"I cand talk ride," I said. It was as if my tongue were still sleeping in the bed of my mouth. "Whad day is it?"

"It is still Wednesday." She looked at the bright digital clock on the wall. "Nope. Thursday morning. I think we will be going home today. The tests are over for now."

"Mudder, I really cand talk ride. Whad did dey find oud?"

"I guess we are going to discuss it with the neurologist this morning. Your speech is probably slow because of the sedation. Don't worry. It will wear off."

When the day broke, the neurologist made his rounds and reported that they had not found anything unusual on any of the tests. He dismissed the slurred speech as a result of the medication. We could expect it to wear off in an hour, he said.

Then he speculated offhandedly that my symptoms and sensations might be a result of depression. When he prescribed Prozac, it suddenly made sense. The headache, dizziness, burning, and numbness—even the blindness—were all subjective. Two separate visits for neurological testing and blood work had revealed nothing measurable. The neurologist thought it was all in my head ... in the figurative, not the literal, sense.

I felt defeated.

We checked out and drove home at twilight, and I insisted to my mother that I *never* was going to go to a hospital again. When I said it, she could hardly understand me because my speech was still slurred.

FIFTEEN 15

Saturday, February 26, 1994

I **TOOK ONE PROZAC PILL** and later threw the bottle in the trash.
Yes, I was angry and confused, but I was not depressed. The
months preceding my frightening sensations had been some of
the most exciting and rewarding I had experienced. Having tar-
geted broadcast journalism, I was zeroing in on my career goal.
I had a plethora of friends, a fun job, and a full schedule. My
symptoms were physical, not psychological.

It was clear that I would not return to the university for a few
more days. Dizziness made that impossible. I could not imagine
making my way across campus to go to class; I could not even make
it to my new room on the second floor of our house. It was dangerous to negotiate stairs while I was that physically compromised.

"I jusd need resd," I complained, crawling under the covers of
Mother's king-size bed downstairs. "I don't n-need these meds. I
don't n-need these tests. I jusd need to s-sleep. Nobody will led

me s-sleep."

When we had left the hospital on Thursday, we had made a follow-up appointment for Monday. The entire weekend, I wore pajamas and a robe and lay in a stupor. My mother brought thin soup to the bedside table. Hours passed while I slept. I only rose to go to the bathroom or to sip a spoonful, and for both endeavors, I required assistance. I could not sit up or walk by myself. Day became night and night became day. Time did not matter; I only stayed in bed.

Many friends called, but I would not take the phone. I did not want them to hear my slurred speech. My mother put the receiver up to my face and begged me to speak to my friends; she was hoping that a conversation would cheer me on to recovery. I tearfully turned my head and pressed my lips together like they were superglued shut. After a few seconds of holding the phone to my ear, she gave up.

"She is not feeling well, Becky. Can I have her call you back tomorrow?" Then she would hang up and implore me, "Please, Nika. Your friends are so worried. When the next one calls, forget your embarrassment about the way you sound. It will do you some good to talk to the people who care about you."

My father was the only one who never called me. And my mother did not even bother to leave a message she knew he would not return.

Monday, February 28
My mother and I fought because I would not don a pair of jeans before going to the doctor. I was not thinking clearly. I argued that I could shuffle into the office in slippers and a robe. Finally,

she threw the jeans at my chest and insisted that I wear them, and then she left the room to make breakfast. I could not put them on without her help, but I refused to ask for it. When she walked back in the bedroom, I was seated on the side of the bed, trying to drag my limp foot into the leg of the jeans, one centimeter at a time.

The anger and frustration were difficult for her to read. When I would argue, even with stifled speech, I seemed like my old self, ready to fight. Then her heart would melt to see her twenty-year-old daughter struggling to dress as if she were a helpless toddler. Mom was in a daily quandary about how to handle our strange situation. She helped me get ready, and we left for the appointment.

At the office, the rheumatologist was walking down the hall as I stood, leaning hard against the wall and staring at the floor. My mother was checking in at the front desk.

"Are you all right?" he questioned, taking my wrist.

"Yed. Jusd a liddle dizzy."

"Get to a chair right now, Nika." He motioned to someone at the desk and draped my arm over his shoulder before leading me into the examination room.

He brought in a neurologist to poke my legs and hands with a sharp pin. The neurologist asked many questions and listened to the state of my speech.

"Well, we are going to need to run another battery of tests in a few days, if her condition does not improve," the neurologist said, standing to leave. I could almost see the white flag waving in his hand. He surrendered to the mystery like every doctor before him. He did not know what to do.

"Call me on Thursday to let me know how she is doing. If she has not improved by then, we will need to admit her."

At the door, he stopped and turned back to me, "Have you taken that Prozac yet?"

Tuesday, March 1

My mother went back to work, calling to check on me every hour. She had taken off too many days. Mark, a sophomore in high school, had been trying to stay out of everyone's way. Our home was becoming like a weird clinic. He was glad for the eight-hour reprieve that school provided, but the more I deteriorated and the more distracted Mother became, the more his schoolwork suffered. My mother tried to let my father know what was going on with us, but he would not return her phone calls. With illness and relational strain, our family was like a building with no mortar. Day by day, our lives were collapsing before our eyes. My mother tried to hold everything. Her arms were full and heavy with the bricks of a broken family. Sometimes it seemed as if my father carried nothing.

That night she and I made an informal truce, as we realized how much we really needed each other to get through all of this. Her knees buckled, and she landed on the bed in her rumpled business attire. Wearily, she scooted over to me, laying her head on my pillow, just inches from my face. Without my glasses, I could not see her unless she was that close. She closed her eyes and prayed, placing a hand gently on my cheek. Silently, I prayed along with her. I prayed so hard I thought my heart would break. When she finished, we opened our eyes and just looked at each other, her hand still resting on my cheek.

"Mudder, I am scared dis time," I said. Tears brimmed.

"I know, Nika."

"Whad is happening to me?"

From her storehouse of resilience, she spoke calmly. I knew she was afraid. The last doctor's visit had done it. Once again there had been no answers. If medical professionals did not know what was happening to me, who did?

"God is the Great Physician, Nika. He made every cell in your body. I am asking Him to heal you now. He knows exactly what is going on inside of you, no matter what the doctors know ... or don't know. You have suffered long enough; it's about time for improvement. You are going up from here. Maybe this is the worst of it. Yes, you are going up from here."

Then she said something that would become one of those haunting, museum-quality phrases that rest like relics in a family's memory bank.

"Nika, don't worry. This *has* to be the bottom of the pit."

It was not even close.

16 SIXTEEN

Wednesday, March 2

8:00 AM:

Mother went to work again. Because I was significantly worse, she had to fight her hunch to stay home.

"Don worry aboud m-me," I moaned.

The rest of the morning I slept fitfully.

12:30 PM:

Dragging myself out of bed and into the kitchen seemed impossible, but I scraped my shoulder along the side of the wall to stay upright and made it to the table. I struggled with four spoonfuls of soup for a few minutes and then pushed the bowl away.

Next I tried to take a shower, but the same thing happened to me under the water that had happened while I had tried to eat the soup: I was falling to my left side. Over the soup bowl, I could not tell which way was up, and I leaned far to the left, almost tipping out of the kitchen chair. Then in the cloud of shower steam, it was worse. My balance was off. I did not possess an accurate sense of space. Toweling dry, I put on clean pajamas and got back into bed.

2:15 PM:
My mother came home from work early. I was too tired to speak and pretended to be asleep.

3:40 PM:
She telephoned the neurologist to tell him I was getting worse. They arranged an appointment for the next morning. After they hung up, an uneasy feeling gnawed at the neurologist. Hours later, he still could not shake a sense of urgency, and he called the rheumatologist to rehash the implications of my medical condition *one more time ...*

5:00 PM:
My fifth-grade teacher, a friend of the family, brought barbecue sandwiches to us for dinner. I ate alone in the bedroom, almost choking on the small bites I took. When Mrs. Collins came into the bedroom to say both hello and good-bye before she left, I erupted into tears. Until then, I had only allowed a narrowing circle of people to see or talk to me. I wanted no one but family to see me in that compromised state, least of all one of my favorite childhood teachers. The strange thing about my crying was that I could not control it. My mouth opened wide, and I made a loud, long whine that sounded almost feline. I could not believe the noise was really coming from me.

Mrs. Collins backed out of the door, apologizing for upsetting me.

"She just doesn't feel well," Mother said, escorting her out. "I am so sorry; I know she would want to see you in other circumstances. She doesn't feel well at all."

No, I did not feel well. I was deathly afraid.

6:20 PM:

Mother was in the master bathroom, getting ready for the Wednesday evening church service. She was a facilitator in a Bible class and rarely missed a chance to meet with other believers every week. My illness had kept her away for a while, so she wanted to try to go and then hurry home directly. Mark walked in the bedroom to tell her that he was leaving for a youth Bible study at a friend's house. The lamps in the bedroom were off, so when he opened the door, the light from the hallway poured in. My eyes had become ultrasensitive, and the beams were piercing to me.

"Close d-door. Too brightd," I said. Breathing was difficult, only enabling me to speak in short gasps.

"OK, OK! I'm leaving, I'm leaving," he said, laughing. After some brotherly teasing about my Neanderthal speech, he shut the door behind him.

6:35 PM:

When she was ready for church, Mother came out of the bathroom and sat on the edge of the bed.

"I don't think I should go to church after all." She sighed, pressing her palm to my forehead. "I have a feeling I need to be here. You are getting worse. I'm glad we are going back to the doctor in the morning."

"No docder."

We sat in confounded silence.

After some time, I said, "Need resd."

"Yes, get some rest. I am going to be in the living room. I'll come to check on you in a little bit," she said. Then she walked out of the bedroom, exhaling her dismay.

8:00 PM:

I woke up with the burning necessity to urinate. It took all my effort to sit up on the side of the bed, and as soon as I did, I realized that I could not stand. My legs would not move. I called out once, as loudly as I could. Then I was shocked when, seconds later, I lost control of my bladder.

"Hurry! Get up off the mattress!" Mom yelled, running over to me and grabbing my hands. She did not know that I could not stand. When she yanked my hands to pull me up to my full height, I swayed forward. The entry to the bathroom was only a few feet from the bed. I thrust one leg to take a step and then another, but fell, face-first, to the floor. My weight was too much for her, and she fell with me. Quickly, she jumped to her feet.

I started to laugh, weakly.

"What on earth are you *doing*!" she spat, thinking that my laughter indicated some joke.

My face was pressed into the carpet, as I lay across the threshold. Waist up, I was in the bathroom. Waist down, I was in the bedroom.

"Cand move," I said, still laughing.

"Why are you *laughing*! Can you get up?" She tried to wedge herself into the door frame so that she could turn my body over.

Neither my arms nor legs would so much as shift. I was exhausted beyond what I had ever felt before, too tired to activate a single muscle. My arms and legs felt like enormous sandbags, impossible to lift. The sensation of being completely unable to move was not causing panic, though. It felt ludicrous, and I laughed almost uncontrollably. My nervous system was going haywire. My body was in shock, and I had no logic or emotional control.

The telephone rang.

The rheumatologist had joined in a duet of concern after ending his afternoon conversation with the neurologist. Still thinking about my worsening malady as he drove home from work, he felt a sudden urgency to call ahead to the hospital. Through what could only be miraculous guidance, he orchestrated direct ICU admission and medicinal orders for me *before* knowing of my sudden turn for the worse. Then he called us to tell us we would be spending the night there. He had no idea I was lying on the floor.

"Hello, Mrs. Maples. How is Nika doing?" the doctor asked compassionately when Mom answered the phone.

"She's on the bathroom floor and cannot move! She's laughing hysterically, but she can hardly speak!" she said, panting.

"What?" he said, surprised. "Mrs. Maples, you must get her to the ICU immediately!"

"I'm sure she won't go ..."

I could sense that they were making a plan to take me to the hospital, so I barked, "No!"

Mother did not know what to do. "Did you hear her? I told you; she doesn't want to go."

"Put Nika on the phone!" he commanded her. He wanted to elicit my cooperation and was sure a word from him could convince me of the desperate hour we were facing.

Mother leaned over me and forced the phone past the door frame, up to my ear.

"Nika! Nika, can you hear me?" he said.

"Yesd."

"Can you move?"

"No."

"You need to get to the hospital right away. Do you understand?"

"No hospidal."

"Listen, Nika, you are very, very sick. You need to go to the hospital immediately. We are losing time. Can you understand what I am telling you? *We are losing time!*"

For a second, it was quiet.

"Nika! Nika!"

"No," I gasped weakly, slowly losing my grip on consciousness.

"No? You are lying on the bathroom floor; look at yourself! *Listen* to me! Listen!"

"No needlesd. No."

"Look at yourself!" he shouted as he drove. "You are deteriorating!"

"No ER." I despised the nightmarish wait at the emergency room. Throughout my life, we had sat there countless hours. I wanted to call an end to the pattern, whatever might result.

"I am *not* talking about the ER this time, Nika. I already called and made arrangements at the hospital before I called you. We might not have much time left at this point. We have to move fast. You are being admitted directly to the ICU. I am turn-ing the car around right now. I will meet you there. I am turning my car around! Now, go!"

I did not answer.

"Nika!" he cried out, fear in his voice.

"OK." I stopped resisting.

After she tried one more time to dislodge me from the thresh-old, my mother called Mark at his friend's house. Standing six feet five with the build of a linebacker, his towering stature could maneuver my weight easily. When he came to the phone, she vaguely told him that he would have to carry me to the car for a trip to the hospital. Before hearing an explanation, he bolted from the house, got behind the wheel, and ripped out of the neighborhood. He did not know the nature of the situation he would find at home. Behind him, his teenage friends dropped to their knees to pray.

I had one sudden surge of energy and started rolling myself over. My mother acted quickly.

"Here, Nika! Here, grab my hands!" She gripped my wrists, and I held to hers. We managed to swing my torso out of the bathroom, so that I was lying on my back, parallel to the bed.

Suddenly, I was paralyzed again. This time I could not speak or laugh either.

"Nika?"

I did not answer.

Seated over me on the bed, my mother watched the color drain from my face. "You are turning very white, Nika. Oh, when is Mark going to get here ... when ... Do I need to ...?" she trailed off, grabbing the phone. She waited for a moment, then hung up. Seconds later, she jerked it from the cradle again.

"911 Emergency," I heard the operator answer in a tinny voice.

My mother began, breathless, "Hello, yes! I need help. My twenty-year-old daughter has lupus and is lying on the floor, completely still. She is not moving or speaking. She is losing color. I spoke with her doctor, and he said we have to get her to ICU immediately. They are expecting her there." I heard the operator ask her a question, and she paused for a fraction of a second before answering.

"Yes. She's still breathing."

Within seconds, the sirens were singing.

17 SEVENTEEN

A VICIOUS MUSCLE CRAMP RIPPED through my right shoulder. Like a vise, it clenched tighter until I thought I might pass out. The ICU bustled with people, but none of them knew the sense of alarm I felt.

Get it out, get it out for me! Rub my shoulder! I can't take it!

Slowly the cramp eased, but my shoulder was sore for a few hours. I knew it had been a few hours because I kept time by the nurses' visits. They came to check vital signs in thirty-minute intervals, so every other nurse marked one hour. Because they always happened to announce the time aloud in the morning, I had a point of origin from which to grope my way through the day. But sometimes they were running late, and I lost track.

Then they brought me a better way to tell time. It was a "clock" I could lay on: a motorized bed. Turning my body manually every two hours was challenging, what with the need to prop my entire length on pillows, so that I would not flop back to the bed from my side. They needed another way to keep fluids from settling within my skin. Nurses transferred me to an air-pump mattress on my fifth day in the ICU. The vinyl mattress had two interior channels, which filled with air independently. Both sides were at capacity when nurses slid my limp body onto the new bed.

"We can set it to shift as often as needed," the nurse said to my mother, turning a dial at the foot of the bed. "Fifteen minutes. There we go."

Fifteen minutes later, the left side of the mattress slowly deflated, and I rolled onto my left side. Another fifteen minutes passed, and the pumps filled the left channel with air, letting me return to my back for a while. Later the right channel emptied with a metered *whoosh* of air, and I rolled to the right. The process was very handy for monitoring the passage of the day and was a lot more comfortable than being turned by hand. However, it did not help enough.

Intense aches overcame me. The only time I had felt anything like them before was when I had been seated in a stiff chair in church or class with my legs crossed at the knees. After a little while, there always was an urge to move, and I would uncross and switch. But if there were some reason I had to wait—maybe five extra minutes—my legs would cry for movement through a dull, moaning pain. This time, I was not waiting five extra minutes, though. The minutes had turned into days. No one effectively can describe the way the human body battles immobility.

Cramps tore through my limbs with regularity. They were the kind that used to send me flying out of the bed in the middle of the night like a pilot in an ejector seat. I used to walk it out, walk it out, walk it out. I never wondered what would happen if I did not walk it out. I always did.

Now I knew what would happen. The sting intensified along with the strength of the cramp. And the strength of the cramp was unbearable. I saw stars behind my eyelids. My body actually bowed up on its own, arching my back and pushing my shoulder off the air mattress. I was not moving myself purposefully. The hard contraction of the muscle threw me forward. This uncontrolled action was a lifesaver, because when the nurses or my mother would see it happening, they would search my back and limbs for a seizing muscular knot, then rub it out. So with tentative effort, I tried to be thankful for that one thing.

I had plenty of opportunities to practice gratitude in that way. The pain and subsequent rolling action happened again and again.

The rheumatologist on call came by my room on his hospital rounds.

"Mrs. Maples," he spoke carefully to my mother, "all of us have been discussing your daughter's condition, and her situation has touched my heart in a special way. I went to Mass this morning, lit a candle, and spent a good while praying for her. I just …"—his voiced thickened with emotion—"I just thought you should know."

He was among countless others who were praying. I wanted them to stop.

There I was, holding my breath again and again—the only intentional action I could take. I was determined to drown myself in death, but the waiting room brimmed with family and friends who kept floating lily pads beneath my feet so that I would not sink. Step by step, I landed on another prayer.

I am still here because of them. They are the reason God brought me back.

I knew it. It was as if they were shouting, "We won't let you go!"

I love the biblical account of a paralyzed man who experiences the joy of walking again. When he does, it is because of his friends' faith, not because of his own.

His friends find the house where Jesus is speaking to a wall-to-wall crowd, and when they cannot wrangle their way through the maze of people, they doggedly carry their helpless brother on a mat up to the roof.

Then they literally dig through the roof, because they have decided that nothing will stop them from getting to Jesus today.

I guess as a child, I always had imagined them digging quietly and respectfully, so as not to interrupt Jesus' sermon or to disturb his audience. But digging through a roof is no serene task, and the point was to cause a stir. They knew this was their one and only chance to save their friend. They were digging in a fever, literally tearing the house apart! They were not trying to avoid interrupting; it was their primary goal. They desired the Lord's immediate and undivided attention. They wanted to turn His face to their need. Right then.

Sweltering in the sun, they dig. Scratching clay with dull fingernails, they dig. Gritting teeth, breathing heavily, they dig. They dig. Sweating. They dig! Refusing to be refused. They dig! It is a raucous scene; they cry out to the Lord, who is just beyond their reach.

They yell for Him!

"Jesus, we need you! Jesus! Can you hear us? Here we come!"

So close; so far. They must get to the Healer; they dig into their hope, they dig into their faith, they dig into the presence of God. They dig!

When they have broken through to the inside, they do not slow their pace. The crowd below falls to a hush; brazen faith is always shocking. On the roof, the volume escalates.

"We're in! Grab the ropes!"

"Wait, is it wide enough?"

"The ropes! We can make it!"

"Hey, coming down! Clear out below!"

"Friend, are you ready? This is it. We've got you. On three ... One ... two ..."

The man on the mat holds his shaking breath. The friends look at one another and synchronize their resolve. There is no turning back now.

"Three ...*Go! Go, go, go!*"

While a stupefied crowd looks on, they audaciously lower their dear one through the raw opening they have ripped into the ceiling with bare hands. The crowd below gasps.

Jesus is smiling. He knew they would come today.

"We've got you! We won't let you go!" they shout to their terrified friend, who is hanging on a mat and some rigging in midair. His eyes are scrunched tight.

Muscles strain and tremble. Kneeling, the friends resist against the rough surface of the roof as it tears into flesh. Their hands burn, so tight is their grip.

"We won't let you go!"

Finally, the mat kisses the dirt floor at Jesus' feet. The paralyzed man opens his eyes. On the roof there is sudden silence.

Everyone is paralyzed.

Then, one faint sound. The man on the mat is weeping. He cannot cover his own face or wipe his own eyes, so he closes them in grief. The Lord looks on lovingly and drops Himself down to sit on His ankles. He touches the man's tears with gentle fingers. Jesus looks up.

On the wrecked roof, the persistent friends rise slowly, panting, holding slack ropes. Tears run down dirty cheeks. One of them wipes his dry mouth with the back of his hand. Here is the rugged moment they want so badly; they have wrested the Lord's attention away from the crowd. He has turned His face to their need. They are looking directly into the eyes of the One who loves their friend more than they do. They had expected to beg, but now they cannot speak. Jesus sees their skinned knees, their sweat, their living belief. Action has spoken for them.

The Messiah returns His gaze to the floor and playfully brushes some brittle crumbs of clay from the man's hair. Our Lord cannot contain a hearty laugh. Faith is His pleasure.

And the once-paralyzed man walks out the door.

My own friends stood in the waiting room as if they were on a roof. They held hands to pray together, forming a wreath of faith. Many stayed on their knees. They befriended visitors who had come for other patients and urged them to join as they looked directly *into the eyes of the One who loves their friends more than they do.* Prayer rose heavenward from that waiting room for *all* the patients in the ICU.

"We won't let you go!" they cried.

Word about me spread through churches, across my

Christian college campus, and from friend to friend. Soon, the wreath widened, and we received calls and cards from all over the United States.

God saw reddened knees, sore from praying. He took note of living belief and smiled. He knew they would come.

That night I could not fall asleep. The lines between waking and sleeping blurred. My horizontal position never changed, and excruciating episodes of muscle death reiterated endlessly. The nurses were in and out at all hours. My eyes never opened, so morning meant nothing to me. There was a shaft of light from the window, or there was not. That fact alone signaled night and day.

Still, I needed rest after such intensity, both emotionally and physically. I felt exhausted beyond repair. I knew I could drift off so much easier when someone, Mother, Dad, Mark, or a nurse would hold my hand. That night, I needed my hand to be held more than anything. I was emotionally tortured. I could not fall asleep without it.

The room was quiet. Since I had been in the ICU, Mark had been living at home alone, save short visits to the hospital. Mother crossed her fingers that he went to school on time and could find something to eat in the kitchen pantry. The reality was not quite as idyllic as she imagined. What did she expect? She had given a teenager her gas card. He consumed the same convenience-store meal every night for two weeks straight: a one-liter soda, a hot dog with melted cheese, one large bag of potato chips, a jar of French onion dip, and a king-size pack of peanut butter cups. He was reaching for routine and structure while our lives seemed to be crumbling. The only way he could find it was by eating the exact same thing every night, though he ate in the car or in front of the television alone. He was going to school, although he would drag himself through the entrance at about 10:00 AM.

On that rare night, Dad stayed at home with him. Mother was with me, but she was already asleep. I could not have spoken to her, anyway.

God, I need You. I can't go to sleep tonight ... Will you please send someone to hold my hand? I can't tell anyone what I need, can't ask anyone. Will you please just tell Mom or a nurse or somebody to hold my hand?

A *whoosh* of the mattress slowly sent me to my left side. I waited for relief. Fifteen minutes later, another *whoosh*, and I was evenly on my back, just as someone walked into the room.

The scent of his skin was unfamiliar, but clearly there were soft masculine tones. His steps made no noise; Mother did not even stir. Moments after he entered, I could sense him moving around the bed to take the chair Mark had occupied in the afternoon. The man took my right hand, holding it warmly. I tried to open my eyes, but could not.

Oh, thank you, God! I don't care who this is, maybe that doctor who told Mom he was praying and lighting a candle for me at Mass. Yes! I am sure it's him. Now, just help me to fall asleep quickly before he lets go. Just a couple of hours of sleep tonight, please!

With the dear comfort of someone's touch, I was dozing peacefully before the mattress shifted again.

I enjoyed a short but sound sleep. It was enough; I felt better.

When I awoke, he was still holding my hand. Mother breathed heavily across the room. The light through my eyelids was thin. Dawn.

I had to open my eyes. I had to see my new friend, who had brought with him the gift of much needed rest. I tried twice, and on the second try, my lids gave way and opened. Through my old myopia and newly unstable eyes, I could barely make out the scope of the room in my right periphery. But I knew one thing for sure.

No one was there.

In an instant, the tender pressure on my hand was gone.

EIGHTEEN 18

THEY PREPARED ME FOR LONG-TERM quadriplegia, despite my progress over the critical weekend. I had begun to speak one or two words at a time and could open my eyelids, although I could not see clearly because my eyes still bobbled back and forth separately. It was better to keep them closed.

The doctor ordered a feeding tube, inserted into my nose and traveling down my throat, through my stomach to the opening of my small intestine. Where it lay, my throat burned. I had a weakened ability to swallow, although it was hardly strong enough to keep me from choking on my own saliva. When I did swallow, the feeding tube would rub up and down against my raw esophagus, creating bloody places I could taste.

Twice a day, nurses would part my lips to "brush" my teeth. They rubbed swiftly with a sponge at the end of a small stick. The sponge had been soaked in an ill-tasting hospital mouthwash. There was not much liquid in the inch-long sponge, but as the rivulets ran over my tongue, it was a dual torture. On one hand, the liquid nearly choked me. On the other, my thirst was intense after seven days without a drink, and I needed the drops to relieve my painful, arid mouth. But it was not enough to slake my thirst. Just enough to make it worse. Even my lips were dry and cracking, because I could not use my half-paralyzed tongue to moisten them. Toothbrushing always began with a quick swab of mouthwash over my lips. The goal was to dampen them a little. However, when the cool air hit my torn mouth, now wet, it stung brutally.

Therapists created plaster molds of my legs. These were to form customized plastic splints that would hold them in healthy positions, thereby keeping my tendons from contracting sharply, deforming my limbs. A person wears those kinds of splints, they told my mother, when he or she is expected to be immobile for a long time.

Veins that were already weak from chemo and steroids began to betray me. The IV site had been changed five times in as many days, including sites on my ankles and on the tops of my feet. Optimum intravenous sites were completely gone. I regretted the day I had refused the implanted port years before.

One morning, I felt a biting sensation on the inside of my forearm at the IV site. Somebody needed to look at it, immediately, but my hand was under the blanket. The nurse had just left, so it would be another half hour before she returned. Mother had left the room. The burning irritation on my arm was tremendous.

What is happening with the IV?

I tried to think of other things, purposefully reliving memories or listening to conversations in the hall. The agonizing pain spread out to my wrist and toward my elbow. Just when I thought I could not take another minute, the next nurse came. I opened my mouth and spoke. My lips dragged slowly and heavily for my first word, and my throat opened wide when I uttered a sound, creating a slur that was both tight and hollow.

"IV," I said, almost strangled by the feeding tube.

"Oh, hello there!" she said, her surprise undisguised.

"IV."

"What did you say, sweetie?"

"I ... V," I croaked.

"I need? You need what?" The nurse propped the pillow behind my head, making it harder for me to breathe.

"IV."

"Oh! IV!"

She checked the IV site and removed it without delay. "You're infiltrating. Ouch. How could you stand that?"

Because I had no choice.

My vein had destabilized to such an extent that the slow IV drips collected directly under my skin, instead of joining the bloodstream. Liquid pooled there, causing the area to balloon and create a painful dome on my inner arm.

When I finally started speaking during the second week in ICU, I learned that it rarely accomplished anything. I felt like a piece of furniture, not a person whose requests were honored. The more I asked for personal space and dignity, the more I received none. Anyway, I am sure most people wished I had stayed silent. My mood was sour. It is always easy to talk about how we plan to remain steadfast in our faith, but then Suffering actually pulls into the driveway and yanks bags from the trunk, intending an extended visit in our homes. And though it is difficult to be strong during the early stages of Suffering's stay, the real fiery test of our faith does not come until time—sometimes a lot of it—passes. By then, everybody in the house is slamming doors.

Occasionally, I think that if I could have endured physical pain only a little while, I would have been a poster child for faith. But at the point of my paralysis, I had been in near constant arthritic pain for eight years. Add the misery of quadriplegia. The first few hours were uncomfortable, but the more the pain stacked up into days, the more surly I became. I did not want to be anyone's poster child.

If the nurses checked my blood pressure, I ordered, "Leave me ..."—gasp—"alone."

As someone leaned in to kiss or pat my cheeks, "Get out ..."—gasp—"of ..."—gasp—"my face."

When someone was saying something I did not want to hear, "Shut ..."—gasp—"up."

The message was clear: I had had enough.

During a bone-racking muscle cramp, I would try to say, "Rub!" That one was difficult for everyone to understand. Slurred speech prevented my attempts to get help. No matter how many times I said it, no one figured out what I was saying. The other sentences were clear because I had "saved up" for them. I had discovered that if I stopped panicking and trying to move so often and just rested—immobile—while I ticked off about two hours on my mattress, I could speak a sentence or move my right pinkie. If I tried to move constantly, however, I was too exhausted to speak or move at all. That is why I could not communicate clearly when it really counted. The muscle cramps always came without a warning, without time for a deep breath, and their gripping force drained me of energy within seconds.

I started spelling it out, "R!"

"Heart?" a nurse would say, turning to another. "Did she say, 'Heart'?"

"U!"

"You? You who?"

"B!"

"Me? Is that what you are saying? Me?"

The nurses never got it. My determined mother decoded that I was spelling r-u-b after several rounds. They all set about rubbing out the cramps.

Another high-frequency word that was difficult to understand was "head." Most of the time, my bobbing eyes made it seem as if the room were lurching to and fro, making me think I was sliding headfirst off the bed. Even when my eyes were closed, I saw black-and-white patterns moving and flashing. There was a circus of shapes in my skull. The only thing that brought relief was someone's hand on my forehead. My mother had done it accidentally, as she stroked my hair one time. I realized that as long as her hand rested on my head, the rocking sensation eased. From then on, I wanted someone's hand pressed to my forehead at all times.

"Head!" I would cry. When someone complied, it was only for a few minutes before they moved on to other duties, including my mother, who started trying to do a little bit of her neglected office work from the ICU room.

Because I could not move my limbs, I reached outside of myself with anger. Annoyance permeated my thoughts for a while. I was infuriated with my mother for not knowing how to help me more, infuriated with Mark for taking the keys and driving my car (my heart rate would spike suddenly when he walked into the room), and infuriated with nurses for probing and prodding incessantly. Ironically, the one person for whom I had no animosity was my father. He and I had bonded the night he awoke to save my life. I trusted him. I trusted him enough to tell him what I really wanted.

Late one night, I saved my energy and spoke. When I was alone in the room with my father, I said, "Kill ... me."

He had been leaning close, and in an instant, he dropped my hand.

"What?" he whispered, backing away.

"Kill ..."—gasp—"me."

I had seen a television episode in which a character in the hospital died accidentally when an air bubble entered an intravenous line. I had been thinking that an "accidental" air bubble in my IV would be an easy solution. I did not want to live in a torturous situation for the rest of my life, and I did not want to be a constant burden on my family either. I could already sense how taking care of a chronically ill person exhausted everyone. From the ICU bed, I had started thinking that my death was the only way to fix what had been going wrong from the time I was twelve years old.

"No, I won't do that. I cannot do that."

"Please." My words were slow and hardly understandable. I spoke with the same difficulty as a person with severe cerebral palsy.

"I took the Hippocratic oath, Nika," he said flatly. Ironically, it was the only oath he would keep.

Then he walked away. I could hear his boots pacing outside the door for the few tormented minutes until he left. Hours passed before he came back to my bedside. He did not bring up my request again, and neither did I. I know he never would have participated in such a warped plan, but beyond a stoic no, he could not marshal his thoughts. He had no life-giving words to offer to one who wanted to die. My father did not seek anywhere but within himself to find words to say. Admittedly, it was one of the most difficult moments he has faced with me. Any father, doctor or otherwise, would be shocked to engage in such a critical conversation with his child.

Parents have to ask heaven for help. I am convinced that all of us can see the right thing to do hovering out on the horizon, but getting there is another matter. The only way any of us can master the obstacle courses of our obtuse human nature is to abide in Christ. The moment we slacken the strings that tie us to Christ, we create distance from wisdom itself. Christ is always the Answer. Without Him, our own spoken answers do not come easily or with grace. That is why staying in communion with the Lord is the essential task of the parent. We must align ourselves with Jesus. Our children will ask us heart-wrenching questions, guaranteed. How will we know what to say? The difference between life-giving words and words that are insubstantial and empty is wisdom. Wisdom comes only from Him. He *is* wisdom.

I am convinced that an abiding relationship with Christ is the only difference between my parents' responses to me. So many times during my extended period of physical suffering, my mother offered advice drenched in godly truth and carrying a spiritual anointing that healed my heart. This is not because she is some kind of saint. She would be the first to tell you that such a description is far from accurate. No, she could answer with wisdom precisely because she knew she was not a perfect parent. She was desperate for Jesus to help her do it. So He did.

She asked. And because He is the Answer, he gave her Himself.

Parents, for your children's sake, ask Him.

At 4:00 AM, I vomited the feeding tube. Mother had to prop my body in her arms until the nurses came running. My head flopped forward. Like a shoelace runs through silver eyelets, the feeding tube entered my nose and exited my mouth. When they pulled the length of it out of my face, it was murderous, but I consoled myself with the fact that the feeding tube was gone. Finally, finally, I had gotten something I wanted.

After nurses had cleaned and redressed me, Mother leaned in close to whisper a prayer.

"Try to go back to sleep," she said.

For the first time, tears ran from my eyes. I was so relieved to know I could still cry. I responded with feeble breath, "Why ... me?"

She stroked my cheek, touched my closed eyelids. "Why *not* you?"

I could not reply. If I had been able to speak more than two words at a time, I would have said, *But what good am I here, like this? I cannot do anything worthwhile. I cannot do anything at all!*

"You can still worship the God who loves you, can't you?" It was almost as if she had responded after reading my mind. Maybe we knew each other that well. Maybe God was using a mother's intuition to help her comfort her child.

Yes, I guess I can do that, but I ...

"Your purpose on earth is not lost. You can still accomplish that for which you were created: to bring glory to His name. It doesn't take a lot of skill or ability to do that. Bow to Him on the inside and sing, Nika. You can still sing. Sing to Him with all your heart."

I felt such anger. Toward her, toward God, toward lupus and Life, toward everyone and everything. I was not sure I could sing, even if only on the inside.

In a biting memory, I recalled singing "Take My Life and Let It Be" unreservedly. I had offered Him all of me: my feet, my hands, my voice. Had I truly meant it?

I winced at the nip in my heart.

"Look, I don't care what any doctor says, I have the confidence that God can raise you up out of this bed any time He wants to. He can do it in a heartbeat! But He is allowing you to linger in this state now. We don't know why, but He knows. He has a plan, and it may not be what you think. Believe it. Trust Him and wait. Your situation may not change, but then again, it might. We will worship Him either way. All we have to do is participate in His plan by trusting."

"But—"

"It's bigger than *you*," she said, squeezing my hand tight. "His plan is bigger than you."

Then she slipped out to the waiting room to join the handful of morning visitors who would be arriving soon, visitors who were linked to family and friends around the country, around the world, by lovely, glistening chains of prayer on my behalf.

19
NINETEEN

A PHYSICAL THERAPIST PULLED BACK the blankets and asked me to wiggle my toes. After waiting a few minutes, she worked each one herself, ten times. Then she walked around the bed, exercising my legs and arms in a full range of motion. She is the one who told me that unused muscle atrophies at a rate of 3 percent each day. The cramps I experienced felt like muscle death because they were.

"You have to keep trying to move, Nika. Just keep trying. Can you wiggle your fingers?"

I wrinkled my nose as if to demonstrate to her that I was trying very hard. I was afraid she would go away if she got the impression that I was not trying at all.

The speech therapist was next. I was elated to hear she was coming. For our first session together, she raised the mechanical bed a few degrees for an initial assessment. My equilibrium had become accustomed to a horizontal position. I could endure only a slight elevation, and only for a few minutes. Any longer, and my stomach would have risen into my throat. During that brief time, she spooned a dab of applesauce onto my tongue. It was cool and soothing, suddenly the most exquisite food I had ever tasted. Applesauce as ambrosia.

"Swallow, Nika. Go ahead and swallow," she said, cheering me on.

The cool spoonful slipped toward the back of my tongue. My jiggling eyes widened.

I forgot how to swallow! How can you forget how to swallow! What do I do? I panicked.

The extent of the brain damage not yet determined, we had no way to predict which functions would be impaired. As we later discovered, one side of my esophagus was weaker than the other, making for an asynchronous swallow. My throat worked, unevenly, with a fraction of a second lag time. Each benign bite became a choking hazard. I got the applesauce down, but barely.

Next, she stirred a thickening powder in a cup of grape juice, and we tried again. It was my first drink in six days, but it was the consistency of bad motor oil. I gagged on the foul taste and chunky consistency of it. With great effort, I regained my composure.

"Next ... Coke," I sputtered, and she laughed.

"I think she wants a Coke next time," Rita told my mother when she came into the room.

"Glass ...," I offered.

"Coke in a nice glass instead of this plastic cup?" Rita asked.

"No, she wants Coke in a glass bottle," Mother discerned.

"Yes," I said.

That afternoon, Mark brought a Coca-Cola in a glass bottle and set it on a high shelf. I could not even see it, but he told me it was there. Nurses and therapists mentioned it from time to time when they passed through. The greatest part of me thought I never would be able to drink it, but a bit of my heart was willing to hope that I would.

When I said, "Music," they pressed foam-covered headphones to my ears.

Mother had fished through the backpack I had brought home from college until she found my clunky yellow Sony Walkman and a few cassette tapes. I was excited to listen to music again and almost smiled as Mom gently moved the headphones into place over my ears and started the tape.

Instantly, I wanted the headphones off. Off, off, off. With my ears covered, I was severed, disconnected from the world. I had not expected a feeling of entombment. Trying to get someone's attention, I made noises, tried words, hoping anyone was in the room. But only my voice's inner vibration resonated in my head; I could not hear myself. I was deaf to the heart monitors and sounds from the nurses' station, those sonorous tethers that kept me lashed to reality. Suddenly I was on the ocean. Dizziness rocked me. Mother must have walked out as soon as she put the headphones on; I did not know. I was sea sickening by the minute.

Adding to my challenge were the songs themselves. Where I formerly had noticed a warm melody, now I was grief stricken by lyrics. Song after song on the classic rock mix tape cast a flashlight beam in the dark hull of my anguish.

I did not want to "look" at myself or at what was happening to me. The great ship I had boarded at birth had become a leaky raft. It was hard enough to steady my sensibilities, without feeling myself twitch and shake as I sank.

When I said, "Drink," they did not open the Coke; instead they brought ice chips.

"She absolutely *cannot* have a drink," a nurse mandated. "Her mouth and throat are not working properly. She could asphyxiate."

Mark posted ice-chip duty after school. He dropped one ice chip at a time onto the tip of my tongue with a plastic spoon. One chip: melting as it slid to the back of my tongue, gone by the time it reached the desiccated trench of my throat. I opened my mouth again. One chip. Where the feeding tube had cut up through my palate, slurping with great violence, I was sore. I opened my dry mouth again. One chip. The tang of old blood. The ache of thirst. I opened my mouth. One ice chip. Gone.

Later I was the picture of Frankenstein's monster, my scalp slathered in smooth gel and patched with electrodes. Technicians administered an EEG test to get a close look at my brain. In a room with no light, they ratcheted my torso to a 45-degree angle on the reclining wheelchair that they had hoisted me onto with a bed sheet in order to wheel me out of the ICU. I had been lying horizontal for an entire week. My body had forgotten how to compensate for vertical movement. A 90-degree sitting position would have been shocking to all my systems. At just 45 degrees, I pressed my lips closed, trying not to vomit. In the complete darkness required for the test, I could not make sense of the room. There were no walls to me, no ceiling; my body started sliding out of the chair heavily. The technician pulled me back into place before stepping away again.

Then she turned on white strobe lights directly in my eyes.

Flashing.

I felt the churning inside and groaned.

Flashing.

"Open your eyes, please," an aluminum voice sounded from behind the wall.

Flashing.

My stomach roiled. My eyeballs bounced.

Flashing.

"Keep them open," she said.

I felt like an animal in a scientific laboratory.

My body swung, shivering, from a hammock hooked to a giant scale.

"You have lost forty pounds since coming to the ICU, girl," another technician said. I had endured ten full days without a bite of food or sip of liquid.

The top of the MRI cage was inches from my face. Like a specimen on a tray, I held still inside the giant cave so that doctors could achieve another image of my brain. A pop radio station, played for the patient's benefit, sang over the loud, magnetic knocking. Though I do not usually suffer the effects of claustrophobia, the music brought on a suffocation I could not overcome.

"Please be still for us!" alerted a voice over the microphone system.

I was sobbing, inhaling tears with the air. Crying hard, breathing hard, not moving at all.

The tears ran down my cheeks, and I felt their movement (movement!). I cried all the more. The only motions I could set into effect were a few meager words and also ... tears.

One of the technicians eased the tray out of the MRI machine, and spoke close to my face about the importance of being *absolutely* motionless (I did not think that I needed additional lessons). We paused a great length of time before continuing the test. The three technicians stood around the tray, looking down on me, waiting for the paralyzed girl to stop crying on command.

A needle pierced my leg while I was asleep. My leg jumped, and I woke. The needle jabbed me again. My leg jerked and kicked this time. It had been a day or two since my enigmatic verbal skills had returned. In the beginning, it had been excruciating to feel doctors moving all around my body with a needle—"Can you feel this? What about this?"—while I could not reply.

"She is unresponsive," they would mumble, writing on a clipboard. I was writhing emotionally, as if I were a mummy in a sarcophagus trying to scream, *I am here! I feel it!*

Buried alive.

But the sharp jabs now, the new pain that was making my leg kick high under the sheet was deeper. It felt like a needle inserted a full inch into my skin. Sometimes it was a pocketknife. My nerves were waking up, reconnecting, shooting signals to my muscles, to my brain. Each jab was an electrical jolt. Throughout the night, the shocks would move around: upper thigh, calf, ankle ... I could not stay asleep.

When I spoke breathlessly and unevenly about it to the doctor the next morning, I thought he would be disturbed. He was pleased.

"You feel something, Nika. Your legs are kicking, even if you are not moving them voluntarily. These are good signs. Be thankful that you are recovering the sense of touch ... even if what you feel is pain."

I was standing within bayonet's reach of a firing squad of nerves. They stunned me on the soles of my feet and on my knee-caps. It was not easy to form the words, *Thank you ... even for pain*, in my heart. Instead, I wondered about God's purpose for me; I was determined to discover it.

The constant probing. The utter helplessness. Mother had said that my purpose on earth was not lost, even here. Without move-ment or a reasonable measure of speech, I could not guess how God would or could still use me. Prayer was all I could imagine.

He wants me to pray.

Prayer. There is no prerequisite of physical ability or talent to pray. So I began praying for nurses and doctors who walked through my room. I prayed for visitors in the waiting room when Mother mentioned their names. I prayed for her. I prayed for my father and for Mark. I prayed for my church and my school. I exhausted every memory, praying for anyone I could recall. I prayed for people I had not seen in years and never would see again. I prayed without ceasing.

But I did not pray for myself.

Some emotional scratch, like a skip in a record, kept me from asking God for my health to be restored. I decided that He cared more for my heart and soul than He did for my body.

Clearly, the physical body is lower on His list of priorities, I convinced myself. It was the only way I could explain what was

146

happening to me.

I had begun the transformation, feeling so separate from my corporeal being, as I lay languid on the bed. My physical self was a tent with no poles and no pegs. Only my spiritual self was healthy and prospering. But I underestimated God and the fascia with which He connects heart, soul, mind, and bodily strength. Each human being is a glorious network. All the elements of humanity matter to our Creator. That is why He does not ask us to love Him with just one component of ourselves, but with all of who we are. Still I refused to pray for my body, deeming it the lesser part of who I am.

He had to change my mind through a dream.

I am in a hospital. A man is holding me. One of his arms lifts my weak, flaccid shoulders. His other arm is under my knees. My head is thrown back, mouth lifeless, neck arching backward, the ridges of my throat exposed. My feet dangle, moving slightly as he moves.

The man is on his knees.

There is great distress in this cold room. I am in a thin gown, goose-pimpled and unmoving, crippled in his arms. His heart is broken. He is in profile; his own body swaying as he holds mine. It is as if I am his dying child.

His hair is loose, dark, wavy. He wears a long-sleeved, button-down blue shirt and well-worn jeans. I notice that his feet are bare as he kneels, clutching my lifeless body and rocking, rocking.

My long hair swings, and the gown flutters.

He is facing up, straining upward, crying with his eyes closed tightly. His head is thrown back, and his throat is exposed like mine.

"Father! Oh, Father! Heal her body!" Jesus cries out in deep grief.

The word *body* He yells.

I knew then. I am fully loved. He loves my heart, my soul, my mind, *and* my body. He made all of me, and all of me He loves. With my heart, soul, mind, and bodily strength, I am to respond in love toward Him. This is His simple request: give back to Him everything He gave to me. Everything. Finally, I prayed confidently for my own healing.

And then a miracle moved into my heart with joy in its knapsack.

"Hey, I think this is banana pudding on your tray today, Nika," a nurse announced with a laugh. "No vanilla wafers or bananas, of course ... but maybe you can imagine that they are there." She raised the bed and fed me a dull dish of pureed beef stew or some other indistinguishable entrée. I had not been able to recognize any of the special modified dinners the hospital had prepared, so I could not wait for the banana pudding afterward, because I actually knew what it was, and the consistency required for safe consumption was not far removed from its original state. I was smiling inside.

Banana pudding! I never thought I would see the day when banana pudding would be precious to me, almost a delicacy, I mused. *Heaven is banana pudding on my tray!*

I was delighted down to the core. When the nurse fed it to me, I savored every bite, difficult as each one was for me to swallow from someone else's spoon.

She finally assembled the empty containers on the tray. "You gotta sit up a little while longer," she said as she left the room. "I'll come back for you in twenty minutes, or so."

My digestive system was so weak, that nurses wanted to make sure everything I ate stayed down. After each meal, the bed remained raised so that gravity might improve my chances. It was terrible. Internal images—flashes and shadows—catapulted continuously from either side of my temples. Sitting up made me sick. But sitting up was not dangerous, except on the day of that banana pudding.

After everyone left the room, I started sliding.

It was a slow movement, and with my eyes closed and with the raucous shapes in their tribal dance, I did not notice at first. Then I opened my eyes and could not deny that, from the waist up, I was leaning to the left.

"I'm ... falling. Please ... come," I rasped quietly.

My left shoulder fell hard into the bed rail.

"Help," I croaked, hardly any louder. "Help!"

No one could hear me.

My face hit the bed rail, and my upper body swung slightly toward the edge of the bed. I was going to hit the floor and crack my skull. My cheek burned. Because my mouth had been shoved shut by the plastic rail, I could no longer say anything. As my right shoulder dipped forward and over, I felt my heavy hips slip on the sheets.

Help, God! You have got *to save me!*

I was sure I was going to fall out of the bed to my death.

Suddenly, I pictured myself from an aerial view, face jammed into a gargoyle's expression, body tipping toward the floor. I envisioned the nurses rushing in to find my lifeless body, left in a heap on the linoleum.

"Why'd she do it?" one nurse in my imaginary scenario asked.

"Well," another chided, "I think the bigger question is: *how'd* she do it?"

I started to laugh at this idea. Even with my lips smashed, I laughed. Loudly. It hurt. A fact that made the predicament more hilarious to me.

At least I enjoyed my last meal! I continued the "inside" joke.

I laughed and laughed. I could not stop laughing at the preposterous scene.

Am I going to survive a massive, paralyzing stroke and then meet my demise by falling out of bed?

The nurses heard me laughing and came running to my rescue. It might not have happened any other way. I do not know why I could not use my diaphragm to speak at a decent volume, yet I could laugh with great force. Not that my ability to laugh was normal in any way; it was distorted and strange. The nurses had heard me mewing like a cat and thought I was crying or injured. It did almost make me cry just to hear myself sounding that way. Instead, I laughed harder.

This entire experience is reaching ridiculous proportions! Will it never end!

Laughter is, indeed, good for the bones, as Solomon wrote. Laughter saved me from being splattered. Saved my life, literally, just as it always had and would.

On the eleventh day since I really had fallen face-first on the carpet in my mother's bedroom, the head nurse rolled my bed out of the ICU wing and into a regular hospital room on another floor. That was cause for momentous celebration.

Mom grabbed the Coke, popped off the bottle cap like a champagne cork, and invited me to drink ...

Just one tiny sip.

20

"DO YOU SEE THIS BLACK SPOT HERE?"** the doctor said to my mother in the hallway, holding the results of one of the medical assessments for her to see. I was listening, lying on the bed in my room.

"This could be damaged tissue in her brain stem, or it could be dead tissue. We do not know for certain which faculties she will recover until we know the extent of her brain injury—and that will take time. In a year or so, we can conduct these tests again, and if the spots that you see here have changed, if she has regained some movement and function, then those areas of her brain were not dead, only severely damaged. We wait."

Brain damage, the words reverberated in my thoughts.

Brain damage.

When he and the nurses left to continue their rounds, my mother sat in her usual spot in a corner chair. She did not speak to me, but I knew what she was thinking: *brain damage.*

Later, it was time to turn out the lights for bed, and I asked Mom to help me lay on my stomach. Every night, she had been letting the motorized bed stabilize in a horizontal position, and then she would roll me over to my side so that she could rub lotion on my back and my feet in an extra effort to avoid blood clotting and bedsores. My skin would become prickly to the touch; that "asleep" feeling spread everywhere. This time I wanted her to roll me all the way over on my stomach. After almost two weeks, I could not tolerate another minute on my back.

She did not think it was wise, but she heaved my dense weight until I was prostrate on the mattress, head turned to one side. Seconds later, I could not breathe.

"Too heavy ... Can't ... breathe ...," I gasped. My spine, ribs, and back muscles were crushing my weak lungs.

I wheezed while she yanked and pulled, but she couldn't dislodge me from my position. I was as good as beached. I thought I would never inhale again. She urgently called for a nurse and the two of them shifted me to my back.

Only five seconds of freedom ...

Misery had looked me up in the white pages and found my new address in the regular hospital room.

The next morning, I woke up to wetness near my cheek. From the corner of my jiggling eye, I could see a dark spot on my pillow.

"Help ... help!" My father woke and ran to me.

All night long, needlelike nerves had bitten into my arms, slinging them through calisthenics under the sheets. I dimly remembered a knifelike jab that threw my right arm up by my face, causing it to strike the bed rail on the way. I had fallen back asleep, but the IV (now on the back of my hand again) had pressed deeper into my vein and then ripped out. Heparin-thinned blood soaked my pillow until morning.

Desperate not to have that IV restarted, I proved to my doctor that I could take a heaping spoonful of ice chips into my mouth and let them melt without choking (I hardly accomplished this while he watched). They agreed that under careful monitoring for dehydration, I would not have to endure the reinsertion of the IV. They also ordered the removal of my oxygen tubes. Both nostrils were thickly scabbed.

That afternoon, my father was taking a nap in a chair when intense thirst seized me. My breath was gone; I could only whisper his name. It was not loud enough to wake him. With every ounce of energy I could muster, I reached for the nurse button on the bed rail. The "heavy" sheet fell away from my hand. I could not control my forearm as it swayed up off the bed. Like a kite, it seemed to move with the elements, not at my will. Finally, loosely curled fingers grazed the button. With no more energy in reserve, I could not apply the pressure necessary to activate it. My hand fell to the mattress, and I gave up.

Drinking the Coke was my first goal. My second goal is obvious, I told myself. *I have to push that button. Without it, I am helpless.*

I waited and waited, throat burning. By the time my father came to my bedside, I only croaked, "Ice ..." He called the nurse in to feed me frozen grape juice.

As if suddenly reminded of another appointment, he said, "Your mother will be back in a bit. I need to drive home to work a shift at my hospital." Yawning, he walked over to the bed; I could smell the musk of his aftershave.

"Don't go, please ..."

"I'll be back the day after tomorrow, Nika." He patted my bandaged hand.

I would not hear from him again for weeks.

The next time the doctor came to check on me, I was crying.

"Why are you crying?" he said matter-of-factly.

He has to ask?

Without thinking, I strained my voice, "Because I ... can't *move!*"

He touched my shoulder lightly and asked my mother to follow him out in the hall. I could hear him telling her that he would order regular visits from a neuropsychologist to begin immediately. Apparently, I needed help adjusting to my new situation.

When Mom walked back in, I groaned in inward pain.

"I don't ... need doctors ...," I told her. "I *need* ... to move ..."

"I know. They don't know what else to do. He thinks this might help you cope."

"Cope? ... How can ... I cope?"

"Maybe talking about it will help you find some inner strength. But most of your doctors also do not understand that any true strength comes from your spiritual life, from the Lord. They are responding as they were trained in medical school, the only way they know how."

"Mother ..."

She placed her hand on my arm.

"I am afraid ... I will ... never be ... happy again."

"Oh, Nika, that part is up to you."

"Every day ... spoon-fed ... I cannot ... even go ... to the bathroom ... How can I ... be happy ... *this* way?" Bursts of breath propelled every few words.

She sighed.

"I just ... want ... to move ... again."

As she waited by my bedside day after day, my mother had been reading *You Gotta Keep Dancin'* by Tim Hansel. A truth in it had overwhelmed her. She knew she must share it with me.

"Nika, what I am about to say will be very difficult to accept, but I must tell you. If you have to move one inch in order to be happy, you never will be. You never will be, because there will always be one more inch to move. I would say the same thing to you if you were telling me that you needed to reach a certain level of achievement or to receive a certain thing in order to be happy. I would tell you that you never will be satisfied because there always will be one more level to achieve or one more thing to receive. Happiness is born of contentment, and contentment is a choice that you have to make in the here and now. Feeling content when things are pleasant is only a shadow of the real thing. True, deep, abiding contentment is learned right here, where things are painful. Right smack-dab in the middle of your current circumstances. It comes no other way."

If you have to move one inch in order to be happy, you never will be.

It was even more difficult for me to understand than she predicted. Not only was it a challenge to comprehend, I hated the idea.

She was in the cafeteria for a coffee break the next morning when I finally pushed the nurse button on the bed rail. I was gritting my teeth when I did. A nurse came, and I asked her to raise my bed and place the telephone beside me. In therapy, we had been increasing my vertical tolerance by raising the bed higher and higher, for longer lengths of time. I could stomach an 85-degree angle now, for about fifteen minutes. It was long enough to make a phone call.

When the nurse left, I knocked the receiver off the cradle with my wrist. I had planned to try calling a friend. I knew I would not have the strength to press all seven digits in the phone number, but I could press one: zero. After speaking the whole number to the operator, I would have only enough energy to say a word or two to a friend before I would have to drop the receiver in exhaustion, but it would be my first phone call since my stroke. That would be a good start.

I moved my right hand with great concentration, pressing zero with a knuckle. As I reached with unresponsive fingers for the receiver on the bed, I found I could not grip it. My hand felt like one of those treasure cranes in the foyer of a grocery store. Mechanical claws come closer and closer and almost grab the prize ... but not quite.

At long length, I loosely raised the receiver and waited for someone to answer. The operator said hello a few times and then disconnected.

I tried again. Now I had to press the cradle button to hang up the phone before I could begin again. Aiming was more difficult. I pressed zero for the second time, but I was prepared with the receiver in hand by the time the operator picked up.

"Operator. How may I help you?"

"A call ..."

"What number please?"

"817 ... 2 ... 8 ... 1 ..." I took a deep breath before continuing.

"What number please?"

The receiver was too heavy for me to bring to my ear or chin. I had hefted it only as far as my shoulder. My hand swung weakly there, holding the phone, while I tried to speak loudly. "Loudly" for me was the soft voice one might use as a movie is beginning, just above a whisper. I had not realized how hard friends and family were working to understand me.

"817 ... 281 ... 4 ..."

She hung up.

The recording: *If you would like to make a call, please hang up and try again.*

A third time: I pushed the cradle button to hang up. I was losing strength with each attempt. As I felt for the numbers, my awkward fingers pressed several numbers at once. Each time I had to hang up. It was a while before I steadied my index finger enough to press the solitary zero. This time I could only raise the headset to my rib cage. I willed to speak with more force.

"Operator. How may I help you?" she answered.

"Hard to speak ... Make a call ..."

"Are you hurt?"

"No ... Dial for me ... 817 ... 281—"

"I can't hear you, ma'am. Are you hurt?"

"Not hurt ... Please call ... 817—"

"Ma'am, are you there?"

"Dial ... 817—"

"Hello? Is anybody there?"

"Yes ... I'm here ..."

"Hello?"

"I need ... your ... help."

Dial tone.

"Wait ... I'm *here* ..."

My heart was close to combustible when I dropped the

receiver; I was engulfed by such rage. All power had left my hands, or I would have thrown the telephone in pure fury. With my thigh, I pushed it inch by inch until it crashed onto the floor. The dial tone stopped. My anger filled the room like smoke and flame. The fifteen-minute vertical tolerance period had long since passed, and my head tightened as my stomach began to pitch. I needed to be lowered immediately, yet I could not lift my hand to push the bed-rail button to lower the bed, nor could I signal for the nurse. I had exerted too much effort at one time.

Out of breath and out of strength, I yelled inwardly at God.

I do not care about my legs anymore, God! I just want my hands back!

The hallway was busy, but my room was silent save the high-pressured, pulsing heartbeat in my ears.

Would it be so much to ask! Good grief! What could it matter to You? Why can't You give me my hands? Just my hands!

I stopped.

And then a voice: *Why do you need them?*

Stunned, I opened my eyes and waited. What had I heard?

Then again: *Why do you need them? Other hands feed you. Other hands bathe you. You can ask someone to write down your thoughts. Everything you need can be done for you, without your own hands. There is only one reason you need your hands, only one effort that you alone can make. But you refuse to do it. You refuse to lift your hands to praise me. No one, no one can do that for you. You must do it for yourself.*

I listened to the voice that was almost my own thoughts, but mostly another's. I knew I was hearing God. I had never heard His conversational voice before. He was not speaking in a way that anyone else in the room could have heard. It was not like an audible human voice, not like anything I could describe. The words were separate and distinct, but they also were whole impressions without a discernable sound. I heard Him with my heart, not my ears. His admonition was not stern, but loving.

For years I had felt a soft nudge in my spirit to raise my hands in praise as I sang to Him. I refused to do it. Certainly one reason I resisted was that in our church worship assemblies, only one couple, a man and his wife—among three thousand members—lifted their hands. I often stared at them, wondering what could move them so. I was not about to join them in public. But I also did not do it when I was alone, singing in my room, and the reason for that must have been pride.

"What difference does it make?" I said to myself. "I am sincerely singing, even if I do not raise my hands."

Still, I always felt the urge. That little spiritual influence continued, but I did not have the courage to follow-through in action. To someone else, this might have been an absurd inner battle. I am so glad our glorious God meets us where we are and never calls our struggles by ugly names. He is more concerned about delivering us from them.

This time I responded differently.

I hear You, Lord. I will do it. I am not making bargains or trying to trick You into doing anything, but I repent of my self-consciousness. If I ever have the chance to move my hands again, I will praise You with my entire being. Even with my hands.

Heart. Soul. Mind. Strength.

All of me.

21

AFTER SOCKING MYSELF IN THE EYE a few times, I finally scratched my nose.

After spilling a pureed dinner on my gown and down my chin, I finally shoved a spoonful into my mouth.

After sucking air through my nostrils, instead of my lips, dozens of times, I finally remembered how to take a drink through a straw.

After throwing several pieces of paper in the trash, I finally wrote legibly, "I love you."

After nearly collapsing again and again in an attempt to sit on the edge of the bed, I finally balanced there for ten seconds.

After the doctors reviewed my speedy progress over the week, they *finally* said my new room was waiting for me at HealthSouth rehabilitation hospital. They set a time for our transportation that very afternoon. We were packed up and ready to go. But then nurses told my mother that the transport team had gone for the day, and we would not be moving anywhere until tomorrow.

"What! We're not going?" My mother was taken aback.

"No, I'm sorry. We will have to make the transport tomorrow."

My mother acts as if every No wants to be a Yes when he grows up. She asked the nurses if she could transport me herself. At first they said no, but then ...

She signed a few papers releasing the hospital from any responsibility and rehearsed her strategy for getting me out of there. Hospital employees would let us use a wheelchair to get from my room to the parking lot, but they would not be able to help put me in it, they said. I had not even been in a regular wheelchair yet, only a reclining chair. Mom was not sure how to accomplish it. Two old friends happened to be visiting that day.

Mother asked them, "Can you help me get her to the rehabilitation hospital? As in, right now?"

They looked at each other and smiled widely. "We're game."

"We'll strap her in the van. Let's go."

We did not get to the end of the hall before I was sure I was going to die in that chair. There was no support behind my head. It flopped forward and swung like a boxer's speed bag. One friend tried to hold it up as if her hands were a neck brace. In fifteen days, it was the first moment I had left my room in anything other than a hospital bed or reclining chair.

"Whoa!" I warned.

My mother marched before us, fiercely clutching her purse, a small canvas bag of the old clothes I had been wearing in the ambulance, and a few things I had accumulated in the hospital. Her hair was almost blowing behind her at our quick pace. The scene felt like an old rerun of *The Monkees*, like we were hurrying past the information desk on our tiptoes in fast forward.

"Whoa! Ummmfh ..." They realized I was on the verge of throwing up and slowed down.

Mother ran to the parking lot to pull the minivan up to the big glass doors.

In the circular drive, she got out and came around to the passenger side with the car running. They argued, trying to figure out how to get the car door wide enough to pull up the wheelchair and maneuver a human body. It was a comical beginning to my new life. The entire time I was groaning.

"Just step aside!" one friend ordered, pushing the others out of the way and picking me up like a heavy duffel bag, without ceremony. He plopped me in the front seat and buckled me in.

"There," he said triumphantly. "She's ready."

"Ummmfh ...," I answered.

The rehabilitation hospital had said that if we did not arrive before a particular time, no one would be available to move me from the car and admit me to my new room. Mother was not about to risk that possibility.

"Get in!" she yelled. The doors slammed shut, and she stepped on the gas, which slung me to the right so hard my head bounced off the window with a resonant *ping*, and I flew in the opposite direction.

"Hold her!"

My friend reached from behind and pulled me back into place, pressing my back against the front seat, arms dangling at my side. I envisioned that we left smoke rising from the pavement as we drove away. We were in a sitcom. We were *Weekend at Bernie's*, loading uncooperative, dead weight. We were *The Dukes of Hazzard*, burning rubber in the General Lee. Later, Mom would tell me that when I was born, she had left the hospital the same way.

"Give me my baby. I'm going home right now," she had said the first morning, insisting that she be permitted to leave with her infant daughter. "Everyone just reaches a point when she knows it is time to get on with it. Not another day. Not another day," she told me.

Since my stroke, we had spent fifteen days in the general hospital. My mother had decided we would not spend sixteen. Not another day.

When we pulled up to HealthSouth rehabilitation hospital, they were waiting for us. Nurses transferred me from the minivan to a gurney in seconds. They wheeled me to my new room.

I could not let go of this thought: in all the commotion, I had heard a sound I had taken for granted, a sound I had not even thought to miss in the hospital.

I had heard birds singing.

They assigned me to the exit room, which was more like an efficiency apartment than a hospital unit. It was a patient's last stop before leaving for home. It had a small kitchenette in which patients were to practice doing household tasks on their own. Most of the other residents in HealthSouth were quite old, in their eighties and nineties, and it took a long time for them to make it to the exit room. Because of my youth, therapists predicted that progress would be swift. The extra space left my mother an area for a cot. It was a welcomed relief from the chairs she had been using as beds.

That evening, three beige substances jiggled on my dinner plate. Mashed potatoes with gravy, macaroni and cheese, and chicken fingers, all pureed to runny mush. I was ecstatic about the meal. It all tasted exactly like what it was. I recognized each flavor. No more "brown stuff" and "orange stuff" that I could not distinguish.

My mother was right to get me to a rehabilitation hospital as soon as possible. The whole place was designed for recovery. The buttons on the bed rails were bigger and closer to the mattress, so I could press them with ease. The numeric buttons on the phone were enormous and easy to push; I would have no trouble making phone calls.

I could not go to sleep because I was excited and felt hopeful ... and also because my legs ached. In moving to the rehab hospital, I had had to forgo my motorized bed. I woke up my mother at least nine times throughout the night to move my legs for me. Twice I needed a drink and something to eat.

At 6:00 AM, a nurse flipped on the overhead light and pulled back my blankets.

"Time to rise and shine!" she chirped.

"No, it's not," my mother said, escorting her out of the room. We were exhausted from the chaos of our arrival. At 7:00 AM, the nurse came back, looking through my bag for clothes. Mother was putting away her cot.

"Where are the clothes she can wear for therapy?" The nurse straightened up and turned toward my mother.

"She doesn't have any clothes she can wear anymore. She has been wearing hospital gowns since we left home."

"Well, you are going to have to get her some clothes: elastic-waist pants, T-shirts, socks, and Velcro sneakers."

"Wait. Not Velcro ...," I said, listening from where I lay.

"Yes, Velcro. That is what all the patients have, and that is what you will be able to fasten by yourself."

"Not me ... I draw ... the line ... at Velcro."

The nurse talked to us about the therapists and how they would be visiting my room throughout the day to take assessments. I could participate in the assessments from my bed today, she said, but tomorrow I would need real clothing.

When the nurse left, mom picked up her purse. "I am going to buy some of those cheap, easy clothes they want you to try. Enjoy your morning. I will be back in a few hours."

"Mother?" She stopped and looked down into my moving pupils, trying to keep eye contact. "Don't get ... the Velcro ... shoes ... all right? Bring me the ... running shoes ... I bought ... on my birthday."

"*Running* shoes? Oh, Nika ..." She looked at me compassionately, tears filling her eyes.

I tried to train my focus on her face when I said, "I need ... those running shoes, Mother."

22

TWENTY
TWO

MY FINGERS WERE BRANCHES. I rubbed them against one another and felt the scratchy barklike skin. It was thick and rough from such little use. After a month in the rehabilitation hospital, I still could not push myself in a wheelchair or brush my own hair.

I was facing the wall when Teri, my favorite occupational therapist, came in.

"I do not feel like getting up today."

"Come on, now!" she prodded, a big smile on her face. Day after day in the occupational therapy gym, we had developed an enjoyable friendship. But that morning, it was not enough to get me out of bed.

"I don't feel like it."

I had said the same thing to my speech and physical therapists for three days straight. The progress I had made in the general hospital slowed to a painstaking crawl at HealthSouth. Despondency clouded my vision for the future. My mother coaxed me to eat at mealtimes, but I would not swallow much.

She expressed great disappointment that I was not engaging in therapy, but I rolled back to the wall after a few bites.

Then it was Saturday. I spent an entire weekend watching infomercials one after another, and the only industrious thought I had had was to purchase a $500 food blender as soon as I could make a phone call. I did not speak except to ask for a drink or to go to the bathroom.

No therapists were around on the weekends, so I asked my mother to help me into the wheelchair for a trip outside.

It was dusk. The gray city shimmered like a pigeon's neck. Steel and glass business buildings to the east reflected the lavender, copper green, and pink of a dying sky. For a few minutes, I thought we had the lovely panorama to ourselves.

But another man in a wheelchair, pushed by his girlfriend, watched the sunset nearby.

"Hey," I called out.

"Hey."

"What happened to you?" I asked, as if such a curt introductory question were any less offensive coming from a stranger in a wheelchair than from a stranger on her feet.

"Motorcycle accident. You?"

"Stroke. I'm Nika. This is my mother, Carol."

"I'm Louis. This is Diane." His girlfriend pushed him closer, turning slightly to indicate they were already preparing to go inside. The clouds were darkening, and several thick drops of rain fell on our laps.

"How long have you been here, Louis?" Mother asked.

"At HealthSouth? A while. We're leaving for Austin on Monday." I studied his upper body while he spoke. Under a red tank top, his shoulders were well defined. Both arms hulked like cinder blocks; he had fingerless gloves on his hands. His girlfriend was not pushing him for the same reason my mother was pushing me. His girlfriend only pushed him out of affection as they spent time together; he could have bent steel with his biceps. I did not have the strength to push myself at all. Yet I noticed how his sweatpants hung from the chair like they were empty and his feet were small and bent. Two white socks were question marks dangling above the ground.

"Why Austin?"

His girlfriend turned back to face me as she began guiding him out of the coming rain. "The accident severely damaged his spinal cord. In Austin they are doing some new things. Louis is going to walk again, aren't you, Louis?" She patted him on the shoulder as they rolled away. I do not think he answered her, and they did not say good-bye. Clearly, both were on emotional autopilot.

"We should go in now," Mother said softly.

The hoary clouds were still for a moment before tearing open. I was wearing jersey shorts, and the rain stung my legs as Mother hurried across the parking lot.

Just my luck, I complained bitterly. *When I want to take a warm, relaxing break outside that mausoleum of a place, here comes the rain. It's cold. It stings. My socks and shoes are soaking wet.*

Even as I was thinking this, I saw the hospital's electric doors opening for Louis, and I cringed. I knew he could not feel anything on his legs at all. My gaze fell to the concrete involuntarily.

It was a pitiful frame of mind. I knew it. And I did not care.

I had received my penultimate chemo treatment in the ICU, and now it was time for my final dose. For two full years, I had dreamt of this triumphant day but had never imagined that it would come this way. That Monday afternoon, I was too sick to move out of bed, but I was secretly thankful that I had an excuse not to endure another day of physical therapy.

On Tuesday I begrudgingly went to my morning OT session, but I was nauseated and carried an empty trash can in my lap, in case I got sick. Teri had to wash it out three times in the gym; finally, she wheeled me back to my room to lie down. I stayed in bed the rest of the day.

Now it had been a week of avoiding the gym. On Wednesday Teri's assistant came to pick me up for therapy.

"Whatcha doin' starin' at that wall, girl?" he teased.

"I'm tired. I don't ... feel like going to therapy today."

"You wanna talk about it?

"No." I continued to stare at the wall.

"Look, I don't think you are tired as much as you are *sick and tired* of your situation. Would you say I'm on to somethin'?"

I did not roll over to look at him.

"I seen you across the OT gym, mopin', and I been wantin' to say somethin' to you. Guess it'll be now. Here's the thing: Everybody needs to mourn when they lose somethin' important, no doubt. But mournin' will only get you so far. Mournin' and grievin' do nothin' but move you in a circle, and you gonna come right on back to where you started—again and again, if you ain't careful. Wanna get somewhere, you best move in a line, girl. A line. Get up and get on with your life. Move forward."

"Why would I want to move forward ... if I am just going to stay this way," I said to the wall.

"Now see, that's the part you don't get to know about just yet. You might stay this way and you might not. I guess if you lie there in that bed like that, you gonna make all your fear come true, though. You *will* stay this way. You gonna make it true yourself."

He waited, and I was quiet for a minute before I spoke again. "Please ... leave."

When Mother found out that I had skipped another day of therapy, we had an argument. I was irate that she was forcing me to continue therapy; I felt I had been through enough hardship and could not see that she was urging me for my own good. Because I could not speak fast or clearly enough to say to her all I wanted, I swung my fist in frustration, hitting her on the leg.

"Nika, I will serve you as much as I can, but I will not let you mistreat me. I will not."

I swung again, and she moved. The momentum of my arm took me out of the wheelchair; I hurled myself to the floor. Now on my back, I shouted at her to help me into the chair. She walked out of the room and down the hall. On her way past the nurses' station, she alerted them that I needed help. Judy, my favorite nurse, came running.

"What are you doing, baby girl? What are you *doing*?" Judy said, as she lifted me back into the chair. "You gotta keep going. You can't stop now!"

"I'm getting out of here."

Upright again, I pushed the wheelchair foot plates out of the way and slowly scooted the chair with my feet, managing to inch past her and make it all the way to the elevator. I shakily pushed the ground-floor button and then scooted out to the courtyard. Another nurse followed me in stealth.

Once outside, I heard the tech's words in my head.

You best move in a line, girl. A line. Move forward.

Anger beset me. I wanted to rip, to break, to throw something.

Pulling at the armrest of the wheelchair, I worked until I yanked it off. I heaved the armrest a few feet. The small crash echoed up the building's beautiful walls, and the metal skidded across the cement courtyard. When I turned in my wheelchair, I saw the nurse for the first time and balled my fists, fuming. A deep agony circled me like a storm.

"Can't I ever be left ALONE!"

The nurse shook her head.

23

LOLLIPOPS BROUGHT BACK MY LONG-FORSAKEN smile a few weeks later. Using the large-buttoned telephone on my bedside table, I had called Mark. I could speak in much longer sentences now—only rarely was I short of breath—but sometimes my words were difficult to interpret. He had learned to decipher my slurred, garbled verbiage.

"I have an idea, but I need your help, OK?" I was straining to look out the door, making sure no nurses were near when I said it. "I need lollipops," I whispered. "A lot of them. Pretty much a giant bag of lollipops. Giant."

After school the next day, he smuggled a wholesale bag of Tootsie Pops into the hospital like some kind of sweet-tooth's contraband, and I unwrapped a red one right away.

"What are these for anyway?"

"Look, therapy is going too slow. I cannot sit around practicing nonsense syllables, throwing beach balls, and picking up plastic pegs all day and expect to get back to my life anytime soon. I have to have my own plan if I am ever going to get out of here."

"Again ... what are these for?"

"Hand me my running shoes, please." I reached out my arm, trying to snap my rubbery fingers in the general direction of the shoes and then giving up. "The shoes, dude. C'mon." My words ran together like a drunkard's.

He handed them to me. With the Tootsie Pop in my mouth, I tried to speak but coughed on my own saliva. Mark slapped me on the back a few times before I continued, sans cherry lollipop.

"For speech therapy, I am going to lick lollipops every day," I said, clearing my throat, voice raspy. "My cheeks and tongue will get stronger that way. I want to smile evenly with both sides of my face, not with just the right. I mentioned 'lollipop therapy' to my speech therapist, but she told me it was not safe; I might choke."

"Which you just did."

I looked at him, unperturbed. "Guess who's doing it anyway?" I smiled and popped the red sugar globe back in my mouth.

"And ... it's back! The smug face!" he mocked.

"Yep," I said sarcastically.

"Big shot," he whispered under his breath, rolling his eyes. He knew I was still irritated that he had confiscated my car keys while I was in ICU and was continuing to gallivant around DFW on my odometer.

"Aaaaanyway ... I have a plan. For occupational therapy, I am working on tying these until I can do it." I looked at the running shoes in my lap, pulled the shoelaces apart and began.

Later, I would ask him to bring me a guitar and the Bible, as well. I felt like a mafia boss taking care of business from prison. As long as my brother had my car, he might as well run my errands. Teri smiled when she saw the guitar propped up in the corner, days later.

"I didn't know you played the guitar, Nika?"

"I don't." I grinned. "But, as you've noticed, I have some free time on my hands lately. I thought I might develop some new skills while I wait to get back to my *real* life."

She threw her head back and laughed heartily.

"You think I'm kidding, Teri! We are about to take this therapy thing to a whole new level. I have rehabilitation ideas blooming all over my brain."

"What do you have in mind for occupational therapy, then, Little Miss Therapist?" she said in her playful way.

"Look, the things we do in the gym don't look like anything I used to do. Setting a goal like, 'Successfully plug five pegs into the board in five minutes,' has no meaning for me. I want to set goals that are real, that will allow me to do the things I used to do."

"OK, then. You're on. You tell me your goals, and if they are reasonable, I will make them a part of our overall therapy plan."

"Good. Here we go. In real life, I am a seamstress, so in therapy I want to thread the needle on a sewing machine. I am a writer; I want to type the first chapter of a book. I am a believer; I want to turn the pages of a Bible without accidentally ripping them. I am an artist; I want to draw a straight, not shaky, line ..." I went on while Teri listened, her eyes filling as I spoke. She realized I was back.

Emotionally, I had followed the advice of the therapy technician and had stepped off of the circular track of a mourning mentality. Not only did I want to draw a straight line, I wanted to move forward in one too.

If I had to pinpoint the moment of my cheerful heart's

homecoming, I would say it was a few days after my temper tantrum in the HealthSouth courtyard. I had been in the cafeteria, sulking over a gelatinous blob of macaroni and cheese when a nurse had wheeled in a woman who was smiling wider than anyone else I had seen in weeks. She pointed a crooked finger at me and said, "I want to sit there. Push me over there by that pretty girl."

I turned my head to see who was sitting behind me.

As the nurse eased her wheelchair under the table and applied the brakes, the softly wrinkled woman addressed me, "Honey, excuse me if I stare, but you are so pretty."

"Thank you," I muttered, dropping my eyes to my plate.

Obviously, her stroke has affected her eyes, and she has vision problems.

"You *are*! My goodness, what a pretty girl! By the way, my name is Opal. Opal Schultz," she said, sipping her iced tea.

"I'm Nika."

"Meeka?"

"N-Nika."

"Do you like macaroni and cheese, Nika?"

"Yeah, I guess," I said, resigned.

"Me too! It's my favorite."

We ate the rest of our meal in silence, but every once in a while, out of the corner of my eye, I would catch her looking at me, smiling, and shaking her head.

Back in my room that evening, I was still thinking about Mrs. Schultz, while pensively fingering some potted daisies on my windowsill; they were one of many get-well plants sent by friends.

"Do you think these look all right, Mom? Still fresh?"

"Yes. For what?"

"Tell you later." I placed the daisies in my lap and scooted my wheelchair out to the nurses' station. There I discovered that Opal's room was on my hall. I found it easily. Her name was written in dry-erase marker on the plaque outside her door.

"Mrs. Schultz?" I knocked on the door as I rolled inside the room.

She lifted her head off the pillow where she had been dozing during a rerun of *Gimme a Break!*

"It's Opal, dear." She felt the top of the bedside table blindly.

"I brought you some flowers, ma'am," I said, setting the terracotta pot on the cabinet nearest me and rotating my wheelchair to leave.

"Flowers! Really?" she said, placing her glasses on her nose. "My, they are pretty. Pretty flowers from a pretty girl."

She would not stop saying "pretty." She must have seen that I needed the reiteration like drops of medicine, like tiny pills. I turned back to her bedside and touched her hand, a thick tangle of indigo veins.

"Stay a while and talk to me, won't you?" she asked.

"Sure. For a minute." I looked around her room for signs of her real life: cards, photos, plants from friends. There were none.

"Opal, do you mind if I ask you why you are in the hospital here?"

"Broke my hip. It was awful; I was home alone."

"Home alone?"

"My husband passed two years ago. He would have liked you just like I do. He was an amazing man." Her countenance brightened when she thought of him, and her gaze shifted somewhere in the distance for a moment.

"How so?"

Opal looked at me again. "He was kind, always giving to others. People would always say he was the best Bible teacher around."

"The Bible? Are you a believer? I am too."

"Then you know what I mean when I say that he looked like Jesus."

"Well ... kinda ...," I started.

"Let me tell you about him."

We both smiled.

"I grew up in a family of boys," she began. "They were all mean. My daddy was mean too. They thought that women were nothing at all. Just for cooking and cleaning. But I wanted to drive, you see. I can't tell you how badly I wanted to drive. Do you drive?"

"Yes, ma'am."

Driving crossed my mind for the first time since my stroke. Would I ever be able to drive again? I had not thought to wonder.

"Well, I wanted to drive so badly, but Daddy wouldn't let me. I grew up thinking that women were not allowed to do anything they wanted. I mean, *I* sure couldn't. But in town one day, I bumped right into Henry on the street. I was twenty-three. He was twenty-five. It wasn't long before he started asking me for evening walks and such. I didn't want to trust him. I tried not to. But then do you know what he did?"

"What did he do?" I whispered, leaning forward, pulled into her shimmering memory.

"He knocked on our door one afternoon and asked me to come outside. He took me by the hand and then, right there in front of my daddy and brothers, he opened the driver's side of his car and said, 'You gonna drive this thing, or not?" Opal swallowed hard.

"Oh, Mrs. Schultz ..."

"That night we swerved and cut circles on dirt roads, dust whirling around our windows so thick neither one of us could see. We laughed and laughed, while Henry tried to steady the wheel or navigate our way. He taught me how to drive that night. He set my dream free."

"Then what happened?"

"What else could I do? I married him. And never a day, never a day since he died have I gotten behind the wheel of a car without feeling a lump in my throat or tears in my eyes. Henry was something else." Opal's look toward me was tender, as if she were telling her love story to a grandchild.

"Promise me something, dear."

"What's that?"

"Do what I did. Marry someone who looks like Jesus."

Rumpled cotton curls crested her pale face. Her hands, all knuckles, laced together on her chest. Almost as if retelling such a treasured story had taken all the strength out of her, she said, "I'm tired now, but you can come back tomorrow." She closed her eyes to rest. Her body did not have half the spunk of her heart. Outwardly, she was wasting away. Inwardly, she was being renewed day by day. I could tell. *She* was the pretty one.

I was already out of the door when she said, "Do you know the best part?"

I peered back into the room to see her smiling, lost in adoration.

She sighed before saying, "I get to see him again one day."

Part of my inner healing involved the emotional exercise of sharing flowers and gifts with patients like Opal. In order to focus
on the act of sharing, one must count herself doubly blessed.
Looking around the hospital room, I had only the basics: a few
days worth of comfortable clothing, hairbrush, toothbrush, and
toothpaste. (Since coming to HealthSouth, I was aggravated to
note that I had been reduced to only a few rudimentary hygiene
tasks. No makeup. No curling irons or hair spray. I only had
manual strength long enough to hold a toothbrush. In time, I
started referring to my emesis basin—over which I daily brushed
my teeth in bed—as my *nemesis basin.*) But if a person sets her
mind on sharing, life takes on a different dimension, a new hue.
No matter how disadvantaged you may be, ask yourself, *What
can I share?* You will find plenty.

The octogenarians in every other room on my hall were lonely.
They rarely had visitors. Some of the therapists even doubted
that therapy was having a positive effect, a fact that was present
in their voices. Some patients were not "just passing through" the
hospital. No one had put these patients in the "exit room."

Becky and my other friends drove into town as often as they
could. My phone rang almost every night. If my weeks were dull,
at least a friend or two from church dropped by on the weekends.
A lot of people made their support clear to me. And as a result,
cards were propped on the TV set. Plants and flowers sat on the
bedside table.

Now that I had in mind to reach out to my rehabilitation
community through the act of sharing, I slowly inched over to
the cards on the windowsill. Every card had a pretty image on

the front. All the personal messages from friends were on the inside back of the cards. I thought a moment, then tore one card down the fold. Keep half, give half. It would work.

I started my one-woman warmth campaign at the beginning of my second month at HealthSouth. Armed with these amputated cards and plants, I rolled to a few rooms, dropping in for a visit with the patients. I shared only the front half of my card, and it broke my heart to see that some of these new friends did not even have that much.

Mr. Villa had a lot of cards and photos, however. His large family spilled out into the hallway every night. When I passed by, I would see small children sitting on the bed with him, watching the TV bolted high up on the wall. One afternoon, I brought him a plant when no one was there, and found him crying. He smiled slightly when he saw me and the ivy. Then in an English drenched in Spanish pronunciation, Mr. Villa told me what it felt like to suffer from Parkinson's, and what it felt like to die slowly. I listened, restraining my tears. He held his grandchildren so closely, because he knew he would not see them grow up.

"Be nice to Mr. Villa," I told my favorite nurse, as I passed her in the hallway later. "Everybody had better be extra nice to Mr. Villa."

On another visit, I passed a door plaque that read, "Crites, Myrtle."

"Myrtle? I think I've seen her," I said to myself. She was always making wisecracks about not wanting to exercise. Many times I had had to stifle a snicker in the gym.

"Being around her will cheer me up, for sure." I pushed through Myrtle's door.

She was smiling peacefully and looking at me when I came in.

"Hi, Mrs. Crites. I brought you a little flowering plant. I thought you might like it. It is my favorite one because red is my favorite color ..." I rambled on, placing the blossoms on the counter. I looked back at Mrs. Crites. Her expression had not changed.

"Anyway, I know you are trying to rest. I'll let you get back to that. I had wanted to chat with you a minute; we can do it later, though. Oh! By the way, Teri gave me one of the cookies that you made in OT. They were really good." That was when it occurred to me that in the last two minutes, Mrs. Crites had not moved.

"Mrs. Crites?" She was looking at me, but she did not answer.

"Mrs. Crites!" I said louder. Nothing. I panicked and scooted my chair until I was beside the bed.

Could she be ...

"MRS. CRITES!" I yelled, inches from her staring eyes.

She jumped. "Who's thayer! Who's thayer!" Her West Virginia drawl leapt into the corners like a cat, scared, but still smooth. I noticed that her thick glasses were on her bedside table.

"Oh, sorry," I said, backing up. "I'm Nika. I, um ... brought you that plant."

"Who's thayer, I said?" She still looked terrified. Then I saw that her hearing aids were on the table beside her glasses.

She pressed the nurse button and screamed, "Someone's in here! Someone's in my room!"

Two nurses were with us in a few seconds. I raised my hands in surrender as if I were in a police raid. "I was just giving her a plant! It's over there!" I blurted.

Myrtle continued, "Someone is in here! I was asleep and someone was right here! In my face!"

A nurse took her hand, "We're with you, honey."

The other nurse squatted by my chair, giggling. "She sleeps with her eyes open. The first time I saw it, I almost hit my head on the ceiling, it made me jump so high."

"But someone's in here!" Myrtle was still saying as I rolled back to my room, laughing.

What a delight my older friends were to me! Grief stricken by sudden disability, I had felt totally isolated. Then I took a moment to focus outside of myself and found a chorus of company. The act of sharing had done as much for the giver as it had done for the recipients. Maybe more. That is the synergistic beauty of God's design. He outgives us when we give; He cannot help Himself. He sees our generosity and recognizes that we are nothing more than little kids wanting to be like our daddy, trying on polished loafers with baby feet. Then He rewards our gifts with spiritual gifts of His own, because He has promised that "he who refreshes others will himself be refreshed" (Proverbs 11:25).

Most of the time, I had a Tootsie Pop in my mouth. My speech was getting better every day. While my voice still sounded hoarse and strained, the words became less slurred, more audible. My therapists were not around after five o'clock, and the night nurses never gave my evening lollipop therapy secret away.

"How many licks does it take to get to the Tootsie Roll center of a Tootsie Pop?" they would chime, as I wheeled past them on my way to visit another patient.

At least one nurse was startled when I answered frankly, "It's 1,439 all the way down to the stick."

I rolled away, smiling.

24

TWENTY FOUR

"**I THINK YOU ARE READY FOR** the bars," Donna, my physical therapist, said.

"You mean to w-walk?" I stammered at her suggestion.

"Well, don't get too excited. Today we are going to put our hands on them, get the feel of them, maybe see if you are ready to stand. I don't want you to get the word *walk* in your head, just yet."

Walk was not the only word in my head, but I did not tell her. Also: *Run. Jump. Dance.*

Donna wheeled me over to the side of the gym where the parallel bars waited.

"Gotta go get your gait belt, first. Just a sec'."

While she was gone, I started to cry. Another therapist left her elderly patient stretching safely on the floor mat and ran over to me, wrapping an arm around my shoulders.

"Are you okay?"

I nodded.

She noticed where I was sitting.

"It's the bars, isn't it?"

Again, I nodded.

"Oh, sweetheart ... This is your day." She hugged me and squeezed my knee before jogging back to her patient.

Donna returned. "What's wrong? You're crying! Do you want to do something else today?"

"No! I have been anticipating this day so long, that's all."

Moments later we were in position. Donna stood in front of me, her hands firmly grasping the gait belt around my waist and squatting slightly in order to handle the shift of my weight. We had discussed pushing off from the armrests of my wheelchair and transitioning my handhold. Now it was time to try.

"Ready?"

"Ready, but ..." I hesitated. I wanted my mother to be here to see this.

"Really ready?"

"Um ..." I thought about it only a moment before continuing. She had seen my first steps as a toddler, I reasoned. My *second* first steps were just for me.

"Ready."

I pushed off and transferred my grip from the vinyl armrest to the cold bars, and my weight came crashing down on weakened ankles. They rocked uneasily.

"OK, great! Sit back down!" Donna guided my hips back to my wheelchair.

"That's *all*?" I sat down, panting.

"Wait a second, and we will stand again."

I caught my breath, and then we stood. Again my ankles shook, and the soles of my feet ached. I felt each tiny bone and the connective tissue in my foot widen within my shoes. Donna smiled and moved her steady gaze from my feet to my eyes.

"Good job. Let's sit down now."

I did not sit down, staring straight ahead past Donna.

"Nika ... be careful ..."

I clenched my jaw and slid my left foot an inch.

"Nika ..."

I stood, quivering, and Donna waited. My right foot scraped across the wooden floor. Then my left.

Three steps. That was it.

"Go back!"

"Back? I can't!" I grunted. My legs were quaking, buckling under my weight. "I can't!"

Donna held my gait belt with one hand and reached behind me with the other. She pulled the wheelchair forward just in time for me to fall into it.

"Crash!" Donna laughed at my awkward landing, just glad I had not hit the floor.

She slapped my knee in triumph. "Well?"

"Well ..." I grinned, and a drop of sweat fell off my nose into my mouth.

"Well, well, well." She shook her head, disbelieving.

"I walked."

"You sure did."

We practiced walking with the bars, three or four steps every session. A few days later, she strapped my waist to an enormous rolling machine. My forearms rested on a platform about chest-high. I lumbered around the gym on the giant contraption that allowed me to move with about as much grace as an Imperial Walker in *The Empire Strikes Back*. After only a few days on the Imperial Walker, I graduated to what I nicknamed a Grandma Walker, which did not feel like that much of a graduation, after all. Using that standard aluminum walker, I took a brief visit home one evening, which lasted about three hours. My father drove in to commandeer the kitchen, fixing dinner for our family. My grandparents came over too. I had not seen them in almost three months. We all ignored simple facts like that my mother had to cut up my meal for me as if I were two years old and that I kept choking on the sweet tea.

Teri said my second trip off campus was to be during hospital hours, anywhere I chose.

"What should I choose?" I asked, thrilled to decide.

"Well, the last excursion we took with a young person was to Braum's for ice cream."

Just ice cream?

I had to speak up. I needed something more than just dessert. I needed something sweet to my soul: art. Cheap pastoral scenes or pastel florals lined the hospital hallways like a grocery store's greeting card aisle and were enough to keep anyone in a state of low-grade nausea.

"Can I pick a museum instead?"

I had fine art in mind when I had said it, but the therapists took me to the dinosaur exhibit at the Fort Worth Museum of Science and History instead. It turned out to be apropos. While I looked around from my wheelchair, I could not help feeling a bit like a fossil myself. The world was passing me by while I sat, stone still.

The whole idea of the excursions was to give me practice inter-
acting with the outside world without direct help. Teri and her
assistant fastened my wheelchair into the big, hollow HealthSouth
van, and we left the hospital. When we arrived at our destination,
they lowered me on a motorized lift, and from there, they walked
beside me, observing, as I attempted to reinhabit the land of the
living. These field trips were some of the final assessments for
therapy, to find out exactly what I needed to master before being
dismissed from HealthSouth permanently. I pushed myself in the
wheelchair, purchased tickets for all of us at the window, and tried
to find the handicapped-accessible entrances and exits.

I knew the trip to the museum would be a challenge, but
I never anticipated the nature of that challenge. Just getting
around was hard, but dealing with people was much harder. The
museum docents and guards talked to me as if I were a child.
Children within the exhibit pointed at me and asked questions
of their parents. I had trouble holding myself upright; my speech
was awkward. Also, I was wearing a black eye patch because
my eyes still moved asynchronously. Doctors were trying to
strengthen one eye at a time, in hopes that they would work as
one again. The first half of the day, I wore the patch on my left
eye, the second half, on my right. To anyone seeing me for the
first time, I must have appeared bizarre.

One boy yelled, "Look, Mommy! A pirate!"

Sometimes the adults stared as much as the children did. I
wasn't sure how I would fare after leaving HealthSouth for good.

I knew my fellow patients were familiar with my apprehension.
Though we were not contemporaries, my HealthSouth friends

and I shared a common dependence upon others and the frustration of knowing that we used to move freely. At times, I sensed that we were all in this together. I would shout, "Way to go! You are doing so well!" across the gym, even when I was not sure I was seeing any progress. I knew they needed to hear encouragement as much as I did.

But in a sense, they became more my contemporaries than my friends out on my old college campus. My pace had slowed to an aged speed in the last two months, and my young friends could not have comprehended it. In HealthSouth, however, I felt understood by Mrs. Crites, Mr. Villa, Mrs. Schmidt, Mrs. Schultz, Mrs. Kern, Mr. Martin, and a beautiful French woman named Mrs. Crow, who never tired of telling me about Paris.

One of my favorites was Mr. Odom, who was in the OT gym at the same time I was there with Teri. He would peek over my shoulder to get a look at the needle-working hoop in my fingers. Teri had me working on a cross-stitch of red geraniums in a blue Chinese pot.

"It is so sweet of you to make that for me," he would flirt, winking an old eye at me as his therapist rolled him past.

One day he was eating a snack, talking to a therapist across the gym, and Teri called out, "Whatcha got, Mr. Odom?"

"Fig Newtons! What else?" He had a small stack of them on a clean napkin on his knees.

"Oh, I love those. Haven't had them in forever!" I said, waving at Mr. Odom, then returning to my cross-stitch.

"Push me over there for a minute," he told his therapist. When they saddled up next to my chair, Mr. Odom closed the napkin and extended the small square bundle of cookies.

"For you, my dear."

"Hey, thanks. These sure beat the hospital food we eat around here. I appreciate it."

"The pleasure is mine."

A week later, I realized I had not seen Mr. Odom, and I asked Teri where he had been all day.

"Oh ... I'm so sorry, Nika. I should have told you right away," she said in a somber tone. "He went home this morning."

For a moment, I was terrified by the double meaning in her sentence.

"What? He's ... he's *gone*?"

"He made the transition out of HealthSouth today." She nodded. "He went home."

Oh. HOME.

Clearly, I was relieved. "But, Teri, he never said good-bye."

After a long day of therapy, I made it back to my room, and on my bed lay a brand-new package of Fig Newtons. Taped to the yellow cellophane was a small note.

He had scrawled shakily:

Keep the Faith.
Love, Mr. Odom

THE INSURANCE COMPANY WAS FINISHED with me before I was finished with therapy. A doctor came and told me that, if we did not intervene, I would be leaving next week. Donna and Teri filmed videos of me trying to stand from a wheelchair and grip a walker. They sent the videos to the claims adjuster along with a plea from the head physician at HealthSouth, insisting that I needed continued therapy, and that my prognosis was hopeful. In the video, my neck is still visibly weak, bobbing a bit. My sagging eye patch and trembling thighs make it obvious that I am not ready to be released.

But the negative reply came, nonetheless, and we packed my room that night. After ten days in the ICU, a week in a regular hospital room, and two months at a rehabilitation hospital, I was going home.

The lever faucets and the open-concept floor plan of our new house were tailor-made for my reentry. Pushing the wheelchair from room to room was not as hard as it would have been through narrow door frames, and I could turn on the water by myself. Round knobs would have been impossible for me. Our previous house had a sunken living room and thick carpet. The new house had hardwood floors, so a wheelchair could easily move throughout. We had just moved into that house the week before my stroke, yet it seemed custom-built with disability in mind. A majesty of tiny miracles softened the harshness of our family's trials.

Though I was home, I was not completely without therapeutic resource. After the pitiful reality of our videos, the insurance company had agreed to one more month of outpatient visits. They would support occupational and physical outpatient therapy, but not speech. A taxi shuttled me between our home in the suburbs to the hospital in downtown Fort Worth so that Mom could go back to work.

Every evening, I feverishly worked out my own brand of therapy. Starting with the lollipops, my cornucopia of unique ideas had been beneficial in inpatient therapy, so I was sure I could help myself in outpatient, as well. I pulled up to the stair railing at home as if it were a set of parallel bars. There I would do shallow knee bends. In the kitchen, I would repeat bicep curls with tin cans and later with half gallons of milk, the only weights I had.

But when the month of outpatient therapy ended, I hit a wall of despair and halted my home therapy too. I could still hardly walk with a walker. Mom had been taking me back to church, but when we went, I did not feel connected to anybody. I felt separate, different, strange. Phone calls and visits from friends had lessened considerably. They all were moving on with their lives. I still felt paralyzed.

My sense of separation was not anybody's fault. One of the problems was proximity. The conversations at church were all held about five and a half feet off the ground, where people stand. My ears, however, were somewhere around four feet off the ground, where people sit. Sometimes I could not hear the conversation clearly, much less participate in it, because all the eye contact was at another altitude, as well.

One of the most difficult processes during my home transition was applying for government assistance through Supplemental Security Income. I did not want to do it. I wanted so badly to go back to school and hold down a job within a few months of being dismissed from the hospital. However, my mother had become very familiar with the particulars of living indefinitely with extreme disability. Her work at a nonprofit organization that advocated and provided jobs for persons with disabilities had supplied her with the valuable experience she would need to help us navigate the harsh and complex forest we were going to traverse.

"I hate it, I hate it, I *hate* it! I hate being dependent on anybody, especially the government! This is almost the worst challenge of all. It is humiliating! I want to earn my own way," I told my mother monthly when I received the SSI disbursement, used Medicaid at the doctor's office, spent food stamps at the grocery store, or waited in the crowded, pungent, hot, unsmiling, noisome waiting room at the federal building downtown, only to have my number called two hours after I had pulled it. I hated SSI every time I sat before the desk of a federal employee in a foul mood, as if I had come to beg bread from a sultan.

"I know. I hate it too, Nika. Make a plan to stop it as soon as you are able. But right now, you are twenty years old and cannot walk, can barely use your hands, and have slurred speech. I believe you are going to regain all those capabilities, and I believe you will find a fulfilling occupation that is just right for you, but in the meantime, do not be reluctant to accept this assistance that is reserved for people who are physically impaired beyond employment."

"You just watch how focused I can be! You've seen nothing yet! Now I am more motivated than ever. This aid makes me feel awful, and it will not have to last long. My next goal is to get my driver's license back, so that I can drive myself to work to earn my own wage!" I fought resentment by combating my infirmity with greater vigilance.

There is no beauty in help from an impersonal source. There is no grace. That kind of help is not helpful at all, and I knew it the moment the paper fell into my hands. True assistance, true charity, true sharing is from one heart to another. To a heart within arm's reach. It astonishes me that we, that anyone, would think that federal monies allocated for the poor represent a type of "sharing" among us. Meeting another's needs is only effective when it is personal, when there is the ache of observing a void and the search for a way to respond, to fill it in creative and beneficial ways.

But responding to a need may actually involve a conversation with someone who is *in* need. It may involve a lump in the throat. It may involve time we do not think we have. It may involve sharing our table and toilet with someone who is different from us.

It may involve more than the algebra on our pay stubs.

There is another thing. While man's ability to earn does not determine his worth, I admit that God intended for us to work from the moment He placed us in the Garden of Eden. It is obvious. A garden is the epitome of constant maintenance. Yet, our jobs are the privilege we complain about most. Meaningful occupation both empowers and satisfies us. Federal solutions alone are shackles; the recipient accepts the chains of increased dependence and often surrenders his God-given drive to work, and that is a terrible sentence. Nothing about it is socially just.

Giving must be personal. When individuals and small groups in the church reach out to nourish needs around us, that sharing gives birth to more sharing as the recipient later regains his footing and rises to respond to someone else's need himself. Giving, when done well, is a beautiful transformational spiral. It connects us, bringing liberty—bringing justice—for all.

Generosity must have a face.

26
TWENTY SIX

MARK LEANED, CANTILEVERED ON THE EDGE of the couch, elbows on his knees. Every summer he waited for the first Auburn football game like he used to wait for Christmas when we were kids. The announcer quieted. The crowd began their cheering crescendo as the kicker nodded, then accelerated ...

I'll admit: it was not the best time to ask him to get a drink of water for me, but I asked anyway.

Mark turned.

I paused, thinking.

"Um ... with ice. I forgot to say, 'with ice,'" I offered weakly. Immediately I understood that this, too, was a mistake. For weeks, I had been asking Mom and Mark, friends and family—*everyone*—to get and to do for me. And, to some extent, I had stopped getting and doing for myself. Man's best intentions to improve are derailed by the "dailyness" it requires to facilitate true change.

Then Mark was the one who paused, a broad grin breaking over his face. He shrugged before turning back to the screaming gulf of orange on the screen.

"You've got arms and wheels," he said.

Surprised, I laughed. He laughed too; I could see his shoulders shaking. In a lighthearted way, he had gotten the point across. I had to be reminded to get back into the match. I kept running out of the ring.

As football season began, I was still in a wheelchair some of the time. During the last vestiges of outpatient therapy in May, I finally had used the kind of crutches that snapped on my forearms with gray plastic cuffs. The cuffs were hot and left sweaty, red bracelets on my skin, which became itchy and irritated. I surpassed those walking aids as quickly as I could, moving on to use two four-pronged canes, one in each hand. With these, I looked ridiculous; I could not keep them on the ground. The canes, with their fingerlike prongs, would fly out from my sides, uncontrolled, as if I were a convalescing Edward Scissorhands. The final week of therapy I had tried walking on two standard canes, one in each hand, and that is how I left formal therapy forever—with two canes and a kiss for good luck. Well, not even so much as the kiss.

I did not want to walk with two canes.

Two? You have got to be kidding.

So every day I asked Mother to strap the gait belt around my waist so that I could try walking with one cane ... or none.

Two, no. One, I will do.

My goal had been to walk to the opening of the jet bridge to greet Becky when she returned from her summer mission trip to Bangkok, Thailand. She was going to be away for three months, and I thought that was enough time to pull together a serious mobility plan. I had waved good-bye to her from DFW airport in a wheelchair. I would welcome her home in the same terminal, standing on my own two feet.

The week before her scheduled arrival, I was sitting at the kitchen table, the gait belt buckled in place. Mother and I were just about to practice walking without a cane when the phone rang. She ran to the wall and talked long enough to make me impatient, and when I get impatient, I start taking risks.

Fine. I'll do it myself.

I stood up, free of aid, for the first time.

Mother saw me, and her eyes widened.

I smiled at her while she waved her hands and mouthed, "No! Wait!"

She was almost close enough to grab me, but the phone cord stopped her, and I took a step. I took eight steps, actually, then plopped on the living room couch just as my legs gave way. I was lucky that the kitchen and living room merged as they did.

A week later, Becky was astonished when she walked through the jet bridge, saw my mother wheel me in the chair to greet her, and then—right there in the middle of her family and other friends—I stood up.

She cried. I cried.

It had been different with my father. After the single trip he had made to cook dinner while I was on a home visit from the hospital, I had not seen him again for weeks. He did not know how my mother felt when the weight of constant care had shifted from the nurses' to her shoulders. He did not know of the midnights, of the falling, of the accidents, of the broken things, of the bruises, of the tears, of the falling, of the vomiting, of the swollen joints, of the headaches, of the falling, of the medicine, of the practicing, of the falling, of the waiting, of the trying, of the tripping, of the choking, of the falling, of the incontinence, of the frustration, of the doctors, of the fatigue, and of the falling. He did not know of the difficulty that comes with sculpting a life as a family in a newly disabled mode.

He did not know about the experiences that left me feeling like a feral animal so many times, like when my mother and I were on a long road trip to visit a friend and we stopped for a break at a hamburger joint on the highway. My wheelchair would not fit through the narrow bathroom door, and when I stood, steadying myself with a hand on the door frame, she moved the chair. The door slammed shut on my fingers. When she opened the door, I fell hard. There I was, crawling across the tile, *crawling* on a greasy spoon's filthy bathroom floor, so that I could pull myself up on the sink.

My father did not know that I had walked. He called us one afternoon to tell us he was on his way into town to show us something.

I was sitting at the computer in my mother's bedroom when he burst in, windblown and energetic. He stuck his head in the doorway and greeted me, "It's outside! Come on and see!" And he darted off.

I guess he had not noticed that I was sitting in a regular chair—one without wheels.

Standing, I took my cane, and shakily walked from the bedroom to the back door, which was standing open. My mother and Mark were already outside. They knew I had been anticipating this day.

There was a stone path across the backyard to the driveway where they were waiting, watching for me to come walking through the back door. I teetered with each step and kept my eyes on my feet in complete concentration. I almost lost my balance twice, but steadied myself with an outstretched arm. At the end of the path, I raised my head, exuberant and proud.

He was not watching.

Dad was bustling about, busy with something halfway behind our van. When he looked up and saw me standing at the edge of the yard, he said, "Come here! Look!"

My mother's shocked expression would have stopped him cold, but he did not see her, and she could not bring herself to say a word. She stepped aside, boiling. Mark stepped back too.

It was a minute before I spoke.

"Did you ... did you *see* me?"

"I want *you* to see ... *this!*" He laughed.

When my mother moved, my eyes fell on a brand-new, brilliantly waxed, ivory Honda Gold Wing motorcycle.

"Is she a beauty, or what!" He turned, admiring the bike.

My confidence wilted. He did not acknowledge my victory at all. What was worse, I could see that he had selected transportation for one. To me, this symbolically indicated that the rest of us would not be moving forward with him.

In many ways, the external trauma I had experienced in the ICU was not as devastating, not as critical as the internal trauma I experienced that moment in the driveway. I could have handled much more physical pain before reaching my threshold, but I could not endure one more degree of emotional pain. Had our family been a supportive, thriving team, my heart would have had a cushion. A healthy family softens the blows thrown by a world that is always ready to spar. Outside the home, it stands to reason that pugilists assail us. We cannot expect everyone to be in our corner. But what can shield your heart from a left hook when the boxer is your father?

I am still thinking about that day. I am still thinking about how Mother said, "She just *walked*. Your daughter *walked*." Her ire muted intentionally. I am still thinking about the look of defense on my father's face, as if he had just been scolded in school for giving the incorrect answer.

And I am still thinking about the way that he slightly—very slightly—shrugged.

"I can see that."

I am still thinking about how he wanted to go to the movies to see the newly released *Forrest Gump* after dinner that night, and how Mark quickly had found something else to do, so that it was just me sitting between my angry parents in a dark theater, watching a movie that was achingly long. I am still thinking about the way my mother's unspoken disappointment hovered like fumes over my head. I am still thinking about the scene near the end of the film, the scene that suddenly made my father cry, the scene in which Lieutenant Dan, a double amputee, walks on his prostheses. I am still thinking about the pity and the joy on my father's face, and the way his eyes filled with tears. He gazed compassionately at the screen, while—ironically—blind to me.

I am still thinking about the groan that came up from my furious throat during the closing credits, the groan that became a wail as my parents carried me by either arm out to the car, asking, "What is wrong? What is wrong, Nika?"

And I am still thinking about how I took such pains to get on my knees by my bed late that night to ask the Lord's forgiveness for what I had done while we were sitting in the minivan—my mother driving, my father on the passenger side in front of me. The ponytail he had been nurturing for the better part of a year cascaded from his scalp, hanging under the headrest like a bolo tie in reverse, like something precious.

I am still thinking about the groan that became a wail that became an Apache's war cry when I curled both hands around that ponytail and pulled with all my strength.

Part 2

27

MY DRIVER'S LICENSE WAS THE BEST PART. It was like a thick sheet of gold leaf in my wallet, like a secret ticket I had almost lost. It took me back to the university in the spring, one year after my stroke. I felt as if I were returning to a magical world I had been forced to leave, like walking to the back of the wardrobe and pushing past the overcoats to see the snow.

But things were different when I arrived. I had expected the physical challenges: I wore myself down trying to maintain the same level of mobility I had known, prestroke. And I had expected the emotional challenges: my friends were juniors, and most of them were living off campus, so the dormitory camaraderie was no more. Sometimes when my friends were going out, they would remember to call me, but in a year's time, a lot of new friends had joined our group. There were too many inside jokes I did not know.

I was surprised by the mental challenges, however: it was difficult for me to concentrate in class. The process felt similar to the way airline passengers pseudo listen to a stewardess present the airline's emergency protocol through the headphones they are already playing loudly. They glance at her and know that what she is saying is important, and they hope they have caught the highlights. My professors lectured, and I knew that what they were saying was important, but half the time, I could not process what I was hearing fast enough to transcribe notes onto my legal pad. I was listening through the loud music of my own confusion. Names, dates, locations, facts—and my thoughts—ran together in a torrent that flooded me as some kind of auditory dyslexia. Studying used to be so easy for me. My cognitive processing had changed, and I knew it. I was not the same.

But God had a plan, an intricate one. I found the evidence He left like a bread-crumb trail. One afternoon back in Fort Worth, my mother stopped at a nearby convenience store and recognized a man just before her in line. She could not place where she had seen him and could not let it go. As she walked out to her car, she glanced across the parking lot. The stranger was about to open the door of his vehicle. If he had gotten into a sedan, into a pickup, into a compact car, or into an SUV, she may never have figured it out.

But he got into an ambulance.

"Wait!" Mother yelled.

The man turned, expectant. "Can I help you, ma'am?" he said in a Texas drawl. Suddenly she knew. It was *him*.

Then mother ran to thank my dear EMT—the very man who had ridden in the back of the ambulance with me, keeping me alive. What is most remarkable is that he remembered me, out of hundreds of other emergency patients in the course of a year.

He was able to recount to her several moments from that critical night, seared into his memory.

Then the remarkable morphs into miracle. My mother's chance meeting with the EMT was on the first anniversary of my stroke. March 2. Exactly one year to the day.

God lives outside of time. Yet, because His people are so constrained, so shackled to hours and days, I believe He often uses time to communicate with us, as if in the "language" we know best. It always has thrilled me that in the Exodus 12:40-42, God finally brings the Israelites out of slavery and into freedom on their anniversary.

> Now the length of time the Israelite people lived in Egypt was 430 years. At the end of the 430 years, to the very day, all the LORD's divisions left Egypt. Because the LORD kept vigil that night to bring them out of Egypt, on this night all the Israelites are to keep vigil to honor the LORD for the generations to come.

To the very day. Surely God must hurt when we accuse Him of forgetting us. Not only does He remember, but He holds vigil over our plight ... memorializing the very days that are held in our hearts: deaths, illnesses, accidents, and all kinds of life-changing events. He remembers. Our anniversaries are His too. He was there.

After crying myself to sleep for an entire semester at my former university, I packed up and moved back to Fort Worth, admitting that I had changed and might not be able to jump back into life as I knew it before disability. I had been pouring new wine into old wineskins. I do not even recall withdrawing from my classes. Mother opened the front door when I knocked.

"I dropped out."

"What?"

"I don't fit in anymore. They can't accept who I am now, Mother." Blame is the path of least resistance, and I took it. Our minds so easily digest mistaken ideas when the truth is hard for us to swallow.

The idea that I did not fit in would taunt me like a snickering playmate for another year, while I attended a junior college near home. I still had an important goal, a singular focus: I wanted to complete my bachelor's degree.

Two years after my stroke, I enrolled at a university in Nashville, Tennessee. The idea was to travel to a place where I knew no one, so that I would not have to feel shadowed by the Mannequin. The Mannequin posed, perfectly coiffed, in the broad, glistening window of my memory, where everything in the past looks slimmer, taller, and lovelier. When I peered into that window, I felt like a runway model dispossessed, permanently banished to the cold streets.

I used to live in there. And "In There" is a lot more comfortable than "Out Here."

I could not help but waste time this way, whether large chunks of it in daydreams or small bits in flashes of remembrance. Everything used to be easier. Everything. Now carrying my groceries inside the house became a feat requiring the skill and endurance of Hercules (three times I dropped and broke a mayonnaise jar en route to my front door). Making sense of a one-on-one conversation when there were several others around me was like solving a calculus equation (my superhearing remained for some time, disorienting me by causing me to perceive several surrounding conversations at the same volume as the one in which I was participating). I longed to be the old me the way I used to long for new clothes. I was constantly window shopping in my head.

My one mistake was to think that other people were doing the same thing. Not about themselves. About me. If I learned one thing in Nashville, it is that the rest of the world does not gaze into the window of your life nearly as long or as often as you do. Nobody is pondering you as much as you are.

And maybe your mother.

Before I set up house in Nashville, I was sure, just sure, that other people were comparing me to my past, to who I used to be. But Music City sang another song. I made a plethora of laughing friends. I could not continue to point the finger at others for their lack of acceptance, because I was accepted fully there. Blame is flimsy and will not hold up under scrutiny.

Heartache endured. I was walking through the classic stages of grief and loss. I had lost someone dear to me and could not imagine life without her. She was me. My self as I had known her had passed away. Though it seemed easy to fault others, the only person who was not accepting the new me ... was me. My Nashville friends had no former image for the purpose of comparison. Neither did they think of me as their token handicapped friend. After living there a year and a half, some even told me that my disability was a fact they often forgot, though I did not see how they could. Their love showed me that my friends in Texas had not been comparing me to the past either. They deserved no censure. *I* did. As the realization materialized, I knew there was inner work to do, a confrontation of expectations and disappointment, a renewal of purpose.

Self-reflection was essential, and Nature became the quiet counselor who sat beside me through the process. Some days I would drive around aimlessly with the windows rolled down, inhaling sweet mountain air and trying to figure out how to pull myself out of the abyss. In Nashville, gorgeous foliage overhangs tortuous roads, casting jade shadows in the middle of the day. The splayed brains of Osage oranges assault the asphalt as if mischievous trees were pelting passing cars. Tree branches droop, low and thick, until city chipper trucks lumber through, gorging on wood and clearing the way for motorists. The carrot, lemon, and cherry colors of autumn are as delicious as they look on Tennessee postcards. In a sense, I needed to come to Nashville in order to heal.

Similarly, I knew when it was time to go home.

Having switched my major from broadcast journalism to fine art upon enrolling, I took a ceramics course in order to fulfill the degree requirements. The potter's wheels were in the musty basement of the art building. I tried to make the descent every day, sporting overalls, ready to practice. Our professor wore pointy-toed cowboy boots and jeans as if he were a hail-fellow-well-met Southern type, but his dark artistic sensibility was not as endearing as it was intimidating. He was an excellent artist; that much was obvious. We wanted him to be impressed with our work, but impressing him was a Sisyphean task. Every day we made another soaring attempt to improve, but every day we rolled back to the fact that we were mere novices. His students were captivated by his indifference. So I practiced more on every project. Pottery was not as easy to create as it appeared. I practiced, not to get ahead, but to catch up. Wherever square one was, I was well behind it.

The clay was uncooperative. Still dripping from the slip bucket, the mound made a small splash when I plopped it on the wheel. I centered it. With the wheel in motion, I pressed down and held still, forcing the clay into a stable position, but as soon as I released the pressure, the clay would fly off the wheel and splat on the floor. This was as far as I got for a while. I would walk across the room to scrape my clay off the tiles again and again. Sometimes I would be able to pinch and pull up the clay a few inches, but the form would collapse, and too tired to continue, I would trudge home to throw my muddy overalls into the washing machine for tomorrow, never one step closer to the voluptuous vase in my imagination.

I could not *get* it. My suave professor said he could not get why I could not get it. More practice.

The other problem was the particular type of clay we were using. There were sharp grains of dried and broken pottery infused in our moist, pliable clay to facilitate stronger pieces of pottery. I remember feeling the surge of excitement the first time the professor had wired off a hunk and handed it to me. It had not felt harmful, just full of possibility.

Over time, that clay became a torture device to me, and working on the spinning wheel an exercise I both adored and abhorred. The earthen form was a sandpaper shape beneath my fingers. It was grit moving at 200 rpm against my skin. At first, my palms were raw and sore, but the redness turned into striated abrasions that resembled a kid's skinned knees.

One night I donned my overalls, heading to practice as usual, but this time there were tears on my cheeks. I cried out in my living room as I loaded my backpack.

"Lord, I don't understand why I can't do this! I am trying so hard! I know exactly what I want the clay to become. It could be so amazing, but I never get any closer to the designs in my mind. The clay is a lump when I sit down at the wheel and a lump when I stand up again. It is just a lump, when it could be so much *more*. I wish it would just stay on the wheel so I could work with it!"

So it is with you.

He spoke in my heart, and I froze. In an instant, I knew I had been climbing off His wheel.

After a minute of silence, I sputtered, "When I planned to major in art, Lord, I did it because I enjoy making things beautiful and meaningful. I never dreamed that creating something would hurt me so much! Look at my hands; they are bleeding!"

So it is with me.

He stopped me again. He wanted to create something beautiful out of my life, and I was not letting Him do it. Molding human clay has never been a pain-free process for God. I dropped to my knees and wept.

A few months later, I bought a ticket to Texas and climbed back on the Potter's wheel. Through the airplane's tiny window, I saw the lovely fabric of autumn trees spread out beneath us like Joseph's coat.

28

FORT WORTH DID NOT LAST LONG. Only a few months later, the direction of the wind changed for me. I was enjoying an outdoor brunch with a close friend, listening as he relayed his brief summer adventure living with American missionaries in Bangkok, Thailand. As we left the café, he mentioned that the families were looking for a new teacher for their small school of eight children, grades pre-K through 1. He handed me a description of the position. I had never considered teaching before, but the paper shook in my hands as I realized it was something I might want to do. Reading that description of the teaching position in Thailand felt like reading a love letter. I knew it was meant for me. I held it close, knowing I could not cast aside a message from my Suitor's heart, unanswered.

When God pursues His men, He calls them into His Army.

But when God pursues His women, He calls them into His Arms.

There are days when I am sure God has me raging into battle like Joan of Arc, but most of the time, I would rather be wooed than be a warrior. He knows this and kisses my hair.

Did I feel qualified to teach? No, I had not finished my bachelor's degree. Did I feel excited to live internationally? No, I did not have an interest in traveling to East Asia, *and* I was still having difficulty getting around in my own country, one that is generally more accommodating for people who are disabled. Good thing I did not have to love the idea of Thailand. I loved God, and He had asked me to go, so the equation was pretty simple. I was not going to look my tender Suitor in the eye and turn Him down cold. Not a chance. I wrote an e-mail to the address on the invitation and told them that I was ready to come as soon as possible.

The missionaries suggested that I make a three-week survey trip in October before making my decision. This sounded ominous, but I had already made my choice, so I thought of the survey trip as a formality. My doctor cautioned against all the routine vaccinations that most travelers undergo. I did not receive malaria, yellow fever, typhoid, Japanese encephalitis, hepatitis, tuberculosis, rabies, or any of the standard immunizations for traveling in the developing countries of Southeast Asia. He said that my immune system might react violently and cause a potentially fatal lupus flare-up. He did approve the survey trip, however.

"I think it's a good idea to go for a survey trip first," he said. "By the time you get back in three weeks, you will have changed your mind and will not go through with this."

I smiled.

29

S URPRISINGLY, I HAD AGREED TO COME to Thailand for a long-term stay in spite of more medical warnings in the end. The survey trip had not weakened my determination. I had prayed, read the Bible, and written in my journal every day of the survey trip, writing *yes* at end of days I strongly felt I should come to Thailand and *no* on days I felt I should not. There were more *yeses* than *nos*. On the second to the last night, fears set in; I had firmly written, "No."

Should I really do this, Lord? It looks so dangerous; I am not even stable when I walk. How will I get around? There is even less shade here than in Texas. What will I do? Didn't You mean to call an able-bodied teacher instead of me? Are You even the one calling me to come, or am I pursuing this adventure in my own power? I do not want to do anything apart from You. And I certainly do not want to do anything to exacerbate my illness.

I flipped through my Bible, opening to the passage where I had left off the day before. Jesus walks on water, and his disciples see him weathering a tumultuous sea, remaining upright.

"Lord, if it's you, tell me to come to you on the water," Peter hollers from the boat.

"Come," Jesus answers. He does not tell Peter how it is going to work, or *if* it is going to work. He only invites. (See Matthew 14:27–29.)

In the same way, I felt the Lord inviting me out onto a choppy sea.

Is it really You, Lord?

Come, He answered.

I asked myself a question: did I want to stay in the boat? The choice was to live with splinters or waves beneath my feet. Which would I choose? Suddenly, the dilemma was over. I refuse to live on a frigate. It is all about the ocean.

Though the faucet had been dry for days at a time, and then "water" gurgled forth as brown sludge; though the equatorial sun beat down in rays that were thick enough to sink your hand into; though there was no dog pound, and mutts, some rabid, roamed the streets in droves; though the whole country seemed to have the aroma of dog urine; though I would have to leave Thailand for another Asian country every three months in order to renew a visa that the Thai government had been all too hesitant to render in the first place; though the grocery store sometimes smelled like sewage and the contents of its shelves looked like colorful puzzle pieces I could not put together; though there was no central air conditioning in the three-digit heat; though I knew no one except a small team of three couples, who were brand-new friends to me; though sugar ants covered everything in seconds, so that the legs of all the dining room tables had to sit in small bowls of water in order to deter the pests; though I did not speak the language; and though I could not take any vaccines at all, I shimmied over the ship's gunwale and stepped on the water.

My doctor shook his head and sighed when I told him I was going back for nine months.

"Do you realize how serious this is? You are immune-compromised, and Thailand is a developing country without the resources to treat your complicated condition. And the *sun*. Have you thought about the sun? You are practically allergic to the sun!"

Had I *thought* about the sun? The sun had worried me the most. "I'll wear sunscreen all the time. I'll carry an umbrella everywhere. I can do this."

"I'm not so sure you can protect yourself as much as you think you can. If you sense a flare-up, Nika, if you sense anything at all, do *not* stay in Thailand. Promise me you will get on a flight to Japan as soon as possible. They have the medical expertise to care for you there."

When I returned to Bangkok for my lengthy stay, I brought with me several boxes of school supplies and books. I allowed myself one week to establish the schoolroom as mine. The former teacher had done a great job of collecting bright pillows and visual aids, but the room did not really become a cheery schoolroom until the missionaries painted over the gray walls with sunny yellow. There was a child's kitchen set made of wood, complete with refrigerator, plenty of toys, a long knee-high table for the kids, and a desk for me.

Eight students populated my class: three first-graders, two kindergarteners, and three preschoolers. We arranged the pillows and sat cross-legged on an eight-by-ten-foot blue carpet on the first day, a scorching morning in the middle of January. I was warned that I would not need so much as long sleeves during my stay in the tropical climate of Thailand.

None of the children had a problem with my disability. Early on, one boy asked me, "Miss Nika, why do you walk sideways?" It was the only way he knew how to describe my gait.

"It's a long story, kiddo, but I got real sick, and this is the way I walk now."

"You can't run?"

"Nope."

"You can't ride a bike?"

"Nope."

"What *can* you do?"

"Let's see ... I can play cards."

He smiled. "We can be friends, then," he said, relieved.

Weeks later, a kindergartener and I were lying on our stomachs on the blue carpet, reading a Winnie the Pooh book. She turned her gaze suddenly to me.

"Miss Nika, when we get to heaven, I will be a princess, and you will be able to dance," she said soberly. It was a sudden realization for her.

"That's right," I said.

"And when we all run to Jesus, you will finally run as fast as everybody else, won't you?"

"No." I shook my head. "I'm not so sure I'll run as fast as everybody else, dear."

She looked at me quizzically.

"I will run *faster*."

30

SCRIPTURE TOOK ON RICH NEW DIMENSIONS for me in Asia. More than any other book, Leviticus grew on me. Leviticus! The book I had skipped over most often for its dull lists and stern commands revealed thrilling new facets of God's love when I read it in Thailand. Leviticus suddenly became the link that unified the entire Old and New Testaments in my understanding. Maybe I was able to picture everything vividly because I was in a new place. Geckos hurried up and down the walls in my Bangkok bedroom. Of course I smiled when I read, "If [a gecko or other lizard] falls into a clay pot, everything in it will be unclean, and you must break the pot" (Leviticus 11:33). When I had read that verse in suburban Fort Worth, it did not have meaning beyond its quirkiness, because there are only occasional lizards running around the outside of my air-conditioned house in Texas. In Thailand, however, that biblical command registered as a pain in the neck. Lizards were everywhere! If I had had to hold to that command, I would have been breaking pots all day long! In fact, every detailed list of forbidden practices, every description of unholy behaviors and the corresponding ceremonies of cleanliness intimated these questions: How could anyone live up to all of this? How will we ever survive?

By the time I finally reached the Gospels, I realized that Matthew, Mark, and Luke have been waving their hands from where they sit on the back row of the classroom (John sits on the front row—the teacher's pet). They are shouting, "Oooh! Oooh! Oooh!" with all the dynamism of Arnold Horshack on *Welcome Back, Kotter*. They cannot wait to give the Answer.

I paid attention to every word of Scripture as I read, journeying from cover to cover for the first time. I read Luke 11:9–10: "Ask and it will be given to you; seek and you will find; knock and the door will be opened to you. For everyone who asks receives; he who seeks finds; and to him who knocks, the door will be opened." And John 14:14: "You may ask me for anything in my name, and I will do it." And James 5:14–15: "Is any one of you sick? He should call the elders of the church to pray over him and anoint him with oil in the name of the Lord. And the prayer offered in faith will make the sick person well; the Lord will raise him up."

I looked carefully at each plainspoken verse and believed. The message could not be more straightforward: Ask, receive. Seek, find. The words "I will do it" almost glowed on the page. I had prayed for healing before, but a new "prayer offered in faith" seemed the only thing to do in response to my fresh encounter with Scripture. I told the missionary team that I would like a special evening of prayer for my health and disability. I wanted to be anointed with oil.

One of the men pulled a small vial of oil from the desk drawer and turned to me.

Now anyone who knows me knows that I am not the type to be satisfied with a substitute or with just a little taste of something. I want the real thing; I want the whole thing. When I reviewed David's anointing by Samuel, I did not get the impression that it was a light pinkie touch of oil on the forehead. I wanted to feel what David had felt, to be drenched.

To prepare our hearts, we prayed for a month. Back in Texas, a few classes at church had heard about my sincere request for healing, and they started fasting and praying for me. My old prayer group of girls said they had never prayed harder. And on the chosen evening, I climbed into a bathtub in shorts and a T-shirt, having carefully laced my running shoes, so that I could leap across the freshly scrubbed floor and jog around the block that night. There is no way to describe the depth of my conviction, other than to say that I completely believed that I would limp into the bathtub and leap out.

A couple of Thai babysitters watched the kids downstairs as all six members of the team squeezed as close as they could into the bathroom. I had asked one of the missionaries to be my "Samuel." When I had told him that I desired a real anointing, as David would have experienced it, he had asked a friend who was living in Israel to send a *shofar*—a ram's horn like Jewish leaders would have used to anoint during the biblical era. He emptied a quart of olive oil into the horn and prayed for my healing and that God would bring great blessing to me. I knelt, and he tipped the horn, pouring the oil on my bowed head. The rich, dark fragrance of olives permeated the small bathroom, as the oil ran off my shoulders, coating my legs and arms. I prayed to receive whatever God had in store for me.

It was a moment before I summoned the courage and strength to stand, and when I did, I was dripping. Taking a towel, I thrilled to step over the porcelain edge. Then I felt the recognizable weakness compromising my ankles.

The missionaries were smiling and waiting.

I was smiling too, as I wrapped the towel around my shoulders and limped out of the bathroom. Nothing had changed. The faithful missionaries began singing praises behind me. No matter what, He is our God. No matter what, He is worthy of song.

I had believed. That was what mattered to me. "Without faith it is impossible to please God," the Hebrew writer tells us (Hebrews 11:6). If I had had anything that night, I had had faith. No disabled person in her right mind would kneel in a bathtub slick with oil unless she did not feel the need to negotiate a reasonably safe exit strategy. I had not even thought about the possibility of my slipping and breaking my neck as I tried to stand. I was sure I would jump up and over the bathtub like a hurdler on the track. I know I had enough faith.

As it was, I had climbed out without slipping, and that was a miracle. But that is where the miracles ended for me. At least the visible ones. I remained disabled.

My hair was greasy for almost two weeks. The rancid smell in my clothes never came out, though we washed and washed them. A stream of hot tap water helped my running shoes, but they remained a dark gray from then on.

A lot of people still ask me if they can pray for me, if we should ask for healing one more time, both for my disability and for my chronic illness. But they do not know about that night in the Bangkok bathtub.

On that night, I stopped wondering and worrying about my illness, trying to find some excuse for it, as if God had blinked in 1986 when I was diagnosed with lupus and again in 1994 when I had had my stroke. All those verses about healing and about God's promise to answer earnest prayers might not reconcile with continued illness and disability to some people, but they do to me. God did not ignore me when I prayed. On the contrary, I am sure that He listened intently to my prayers. That night, I did what He said to do: I asked in faith. When He answered, I accepted it.

He must have some kind of plan that is bigger and better, more important, than my being healed, I reasoned.

And if I had learned anything from having recently read the Bible from cover to cover, it is that God always has a plan, and that, most of the time, His plans are so elaborate and intricate that they take a long time to develop. Joseph waited seventeen years. Moses waited forty. Twice. Noah waited one hundred.

We can wait to see the development of our stories too.

On the morning of my departure from Asia, I walked our neighborhood in Phasi Charoen district one last time, swinging my 35 mm camera at my side. Spirit houses peeked above the wide concrete barriers lined with broken bottles that stood between neighbors. Those small spirit-house altars, looking like ornate gold and red birdhouses, had the same tiny plate of bread, the same tiny cup of water that had been placed there the night before. No idol had taken the offering, but the people relentlessly made their sacrifices. How I longed to shout, "Jesus said, 'It is finished!' You can be finished!" But the Thais who did not know Jesus still fed the saffron-robed monks and made visits to Wat Phra Kaew—the Temple of the Emerald Buddha—the most sacred temple in Thailand, sitting in the heart of Bangkok like a corrupt jewel.

I had fallen in love with the Land of Smiles and with all the beautiful, lacquer-haired citizens who earned their country that nickname. I had prayed anxiously so many times while I walked Soi 14 that school year, but this time, I sauntered a poignant farewell blessing and then headed back to grab my suitcases and get in the missionaries' waiting van.

The house across the street from where I stayed was either condemned or under construction that had been halted, I could not tell which. A few destitute Thais had been living in the structure for months. They found a couch and repaired it with duct tape, but possessed no other furniture for their wall-less home. That morning, I stopped to watch a woman inside the gate as she prepared a fish breakfast on a fire in the middle of the littered yard. One woman bathed, her sarong loosely and strategically tied around her chest as she bent to dip a torn rag in a bucket. A man returned with a treasure he had discovered while digging in a ten-gallon trash drum nearby. A man who was squatting to prepare more food in a bowl turned to me. I smiled. He did not smile in return, but nodded as I raised my camera as a question.

In the black-and-white photograph, both the man over the bowl and the woman who is cooking are looking at me. Stacks of two-by-fours and broken glass tower around them. What is not in the photograph is what was happening at my feet as I took the picture. I had only snapped a photo or two when I felt warmth on my right calf. Liquid was running into my shoe. I looked down to see a tall

Dalmatian with hind leg raised, urinating on my leg.

Later I laughed as I tried to imagine what the Thais had been thinking as they watched me taking their picture and being christened for my journey simultaneously.

It was too late to change clothes, of course. My bags were already packed, and besides, I had only one pair of shoes. So I wore the perfume of Thailand on the twenty-two-hour trip home.

31

SLOWNESS IS THE BUTTONLESS COAT on my shoulders, the garment I never remove. Sewn shut, the yoke tightens at times, reminding me that mobility is a luxurious space, in which I must live more narrowly than others. Sometimes I almost think I can disguise my limp, but realize eventually that I cannot. It is part of who I am, like the color of my hair or the place of my birth. I would be psychologically different, I think, had I been born a blonde in Michigan or a redhead in Florida.

The handful of physical descriptors we carry along with us in life do not make us who we are, but other people's responses to those descriptors, coupled with our responses to their responses do, indeed, shape us. Would we take such care in naming our infants if this were not true? We want our male names to be strong. We want our female names to be somewhat softer. We want baby names to be flexible enough to fit a fun-loving child and then grow to fit an adult who needs to be taken seriously.

My conviction that disability is a divinely created part of who I am is central to my view of myself and the world. Continuing to pray against it when the Lord has been clear in letting it remain would be like praying for my eye color to change—as if the hazel He picked for me is nice, but not quite good enough. I do not want to be healed as much as I want God's plan for my life—whether that involves healing or not. My desire for His purposes fuels my constant prayer. Technically, He has guaranteed my healing, and should He choose to do it sooner than Heaven, my shout of praise will be heard from Texas to Egypt. Until then, I will not be disproportionately consumed with the idea that this trial must be lifted from my life.

Sometimes we lose opportunities to play an active role in the kingdom, because we do not like the part we were asked to play. We are so busy praying for specific circumstances to change that we miss our cues and flub our lines. I have started embracing the whole production, as it was written by the masterful Playwright. Like Paul, I have accepted the grace he wrote about in 2 Corinthians 12 after dealing with an unwanted circumstance, a "thorn in the flesh."

> Three times I pleaded with the Lord to take it away from me. But he said to me, "My grace is sufficient for you, for my power is made perfect in weakness." Therefore I will boast all the more gladly about my weaknesses, so that Christ's power may rest on me. That is why, for Christ's sake, I delight in weaknesses, in insults, in hardships, in persecutions, in difficulties. For when I am weak, then I am strong. (Verses 8–10)

Maybe our painful or frustrating situations are there in order to bring a greater mission to us. The world is watching. Oh, that we would joyfully stay on the stage and proclaim that God is enough. Who else could smile through trials—not superficially, but from true joy—except someone who is certain that the Grand Finale is yet to come? If believers always had it easy or always had what they wanted, there would be no real way to prove grace's sufficiency.

I faithfully committed to take my part in God's great mission as I returned to America from Thailand. Of course, I thought I might hear a clear direction or sense an imminent path, but I did not. God seemed to be keeping His plans to Himself. I focused on my schoolwork and finally graduated with a BS in mass communications from Fort Worth's Texas Wesleyan University in 2002, exactly ten years after I began as a freshman. I chose not to walk for graduation. I was afraid I might trip on the stage. Besides, I just wanted to grab that prized diploma from the registrar's office and get going.

But a diploma is not a map, and I still had no idea where I was headed.

I kept quoting Psalm 147:10–11 as I prayed: *His pleasure is not in the strength of the horse, nor his delight in the legs of a man; the Lord delights in those who fear him, who put their hope in his unfailing love.*

That summer I visited a number of doctors. After taking Prednisone for the better part of seventeen years, I had become concerned about taking near-constant doses of steroids. When I visited my rheumatologist, I asked him to help me wean off the Prednisone and also asked him why he had prescribed it for so many years, knowing the irreparable damage it could do to my heart and bones.

"We were trying to ease your debilitating pain, Nika. And there was no other way to control lupus activity."

"But I started these drugs when I was twelve and did not know about the dangerous side effects. Steroids were never a safe option as a long-term plan."

"A long-term plan? To be honest, none of us ever expected you to live as long as you have. There was no long-term plan."

My previously scheduled appointment to see a neurologist happened to be the very next day. I was overwhelmed by what my rheumatologist had said, so during my visit, I asked the neurologist at point-blank range, "Sir, I am twenty-eight years old and still trying to figure out a career path ... It may seem pessimistic, but I feel compelled to ask what kind of life expectancy I can hope for. I mean, no one has told me outright. It is not as if I am coming to pediatricians with my mother anymore. I am a mature woman who is prepared to handle anything you might say. Be honest. What is my life expectancy, having had systemic lupus from age twelve?"

The physician looked at me, turning a silver pen in his fingers.

"You can tell me what age to expect, sir. Please," I begged.

He paused a moment longer before he said, "It was twenty-five."

32

THE BOY WOULD TAKE OFF HIS SHOES in class, they told me, putting his dirty bare feet on the desk in front of him and irritating other students. He would smart-mouth anyone in authority, and because he was quick-witted, he did it in the kind of incisive ways that always landed him in the principal's office. He wore the same red and black flannel shirt like a loose jacket almost every day, and though he changed the T-shirt underneath, the flannel jacket had a signature odor. He tried to sneak junk food from his backpack and eat at his desk at the back of the room.

John had discovered *me* because of his addiction to hard candy, which I kept in a crystal bowl on my desk. He would walk all the way to the back of the middle school office, crack a few stale jokes and take a piece of candy, sometimes three. His fingers appeared to be permanently stained orange from having eaten so many cheesy chips. His tongue was blue from something I knew was garishly sweet.

He was not what you would call popular, but everybody knew him.

In the teachers' lounge, sometimes the long lunch table became a landfill of student stories, as weary educators dumped their frustration. John was always on the bottom of the pile. Not long after I had started working at a public school as the counseling assistant—which was a glorified title for a data-entry clerk—I learned that teachers' lounges can be negative places. I had stopped eating there, preferring to take my sack lunch outside. I needed the peace and quiet in order to reboot for the afternoon. A new wing of the school was being constructed, so I used it as my secret place to get away. I would lean against the red brick of the old wing, sitting on a corner of the concrete slab, resting my feet against the new wood frame and daydreaming during my lunch break. I had to take off one of my shoes and stick it in the glass door, because office aides like me were not issued building keys, and I could not get back inside.

I was watching dust blow off the dry cement one day when it occurred to me that John might need *me* more than anyone else in the school at the moment. The next day, I took my sack lunch to the cafeteria for the first time. There was John, seated at a table by himself, and I asked if I could join him. He was reading a video-gamers' magazine and, other than nodding to allow me to sit, he never acknowledged me. The following Monday, I sat beside him again. Every Monday, I came back.

The only things he ever ate for lunch fell into a junk food category that subsists below burgers and hot dogs. John always ate from the "worse than junk food" category, which features such alarming lunchtime choices as cotton candy in a small convenience-store-sized bag (blue, of course), fried onion chips, and cherry soda. He watched me drinking from a carton of milk and eating a peanut-butter-and-jelly sandwich on wheat bread as if I were some yogi practicing the grueling self-denial of a rigid ascetic lifestyle. When I brought baby carrots, he moaned of torture.

We started having fun, John and I. He told the same jokes I had learned a decade and a half earlier when *I* was in junior high, but I laughed on cue. I listened to him bubble over in the telling of upcoming video-game releases, and feigned interest. Sometimes he talked about his parents, who were incarcerated, and his grandmother, who had become his primary guardian. He did not have to be telling me a particularly poignant story in order to bring tears to his eyes. He changed the subject quickly.

A couple of other boys joined us now and then.

On a Monday in the spring, I was late to the cafeteria. I breezed in and halted. John was surrounded by a group of seven boys, outcasts all, and they were laughing merrily, as if the other tables—populated with lip-gloss prima donnas and hallway quarterbacks—were no more than obstacles in a video game on the Easy level. Clearly, he was not waiting for me. Now John had friends.

He doesn't need me anymore.

I smiled and enjoyed the scene for a minute before slowly walking back to the office. This time, the tears were in *my* eyes.

At the end of the year, the week before school released for the summer, John came back to see me at my desk.

"Broughtcha somethin'," he said, grinning.

"Oh yeah? What?" I stopped typing and leaned on the desk, my chin in my hand.

"This." He plunked a big glass canning jar in front of me. There were a few large leaves and stick inside. Everybody knows: a jar + leaves + a stick = a critter.

"Three of em's named Jack."

"*Three* of them?"

"Yeah. Theys two girls in there too. You can name 'em whatever you want. Gotta go, or I'll be late to math. I hate math." He ran toward the door and then turned as if he forgot something. He scampered back, grabbed a piece of candy, and winked.

"Thanks, John," I said, smiling and peering quickly into the jar before putting it on my bookcase. It was a busy time of year. I was behind on entering schedules for the incoming seventh graders, and I confess that I made a quick mental note to take the jar home with me but promptly forgot about it.

I went home for the weekend. The following Monday was a school holiday. On Tuesday I returned to school and was the first to enter our office.

"Oh no! The jar!" I said, hurrying over to the bookcase. There was no perforated lid, net, or plastic wrap to keep the critters inside, so it was not surprising to see the jar was empty.

I did not want to be a nuisance to the woman with whom I shared the counseling office, but as hard as I searched, I could find no critters. I dreaded her arrival; I would have to explain why there were mysterious pests in the office. I sighed and pulled out my desk chair to take a seat.

There they were.

Five perfect white moths flew up in a frilly column in front of my face before separating and landing throughout the room. One rested on my computer and stayed there until lunch. The others were on tour: the bookcase, an open drawer, the back of a chair. I grinned all day.

John came to see me right after the lunch bell rang.

"You like 'em?"

"Yes, John," I said softly. "I like them very much."

"Well, you been real nice to me. I didn't even know how to tell you thanks. It bein' the end of the year and all, I wanted to get you somethin', but my grandma ain't got nothin'. So what was I gonna do? I thought and thought about it. Then it hit me!"

"What hit you?"

"I was watchin' you walk down the hall. Your legs don't work too good. So I decided I'd get you *wings*."

In that moment, I knew: I *had* to become a teacher.

That summer, I completed alternative certification courses for secondary education and took a position teaching sophomore English, photojournalism, and creative writing. Fossil Ridge High School was an enormous campus, a half mile from end to end. My physicality was stretched to its limits. It was almost as if I could feel my lungs filling with seawater; I was drowning. At my initial teacher in-service workshop, I hoped none of the old pros would notice. Their raised eyebrows told me they did. It was not as if I had not already been thinking that my disability would be a centerpiece on campus. I had confidence that I could earn my students' respect, but I did not know if my colleagues would offer theirs so easily. Before staff development week was over, I could tell a few of them thought the rough-around-the-edges kids in the 5A, Title I high school would eat me alive.

Their fears were not unfounded. On the first day of school, I welcomed each sophomore student with a handshake at the door, handing them individual playing cards. I had devised a seating chart system that required each student to find his matching card taped to a desk and take a seat. The last student to enter would not shake my hand. He did not look like a six-teen-year-old sophomore either. He looked an easy nineteen or twenty. He had pierced his earlobes with inch-and-a-half-wide black gauges he could have stuck his thumb through. Jerking the playing card from me, he looked at it, and flipped it back in my face. An ace of spades.

Teaching and education courses are everywhere, but none of them can prepare you for that moment when the last morning bell rings and you close the door for the *first* time. My new students, thirty-seven of them, stared or muttered as I walked away from the door. They were mostly sitting in their assigned seats. One was sitting at my desk, and one was on the floor, because I had only been issued thirty-five student desks. I made my way from the door to the podium.

"May I have your attention, please?"

Silence.

"My name is Ms. Maples." I smiled. "And I want to welcome you to your sophomore English class ..."

They gave me ten seconds; just ten quiet, focused seconds, before turning to one another, to their makeup compacts, and to their cell phones. I heard a boy in the back row say loudly to his friend, "Why she walk like that?"

I took a deep breath. I had anticipated this and was prepared. My philosophy: why steer away from a topic when you can head for it with a cement roller?

No turning back now.

"You see these?" I said in full voice, pulling two canes, one four-pronged aluminum and one standard wood, from the classroom wardrobe. I dropped the canes to hang on the whiteboard tray with a flourish that made the metal ring, and all the students turned to watch, looking at the swinging canes and then to me.

"I need a volunteer."

Silence.

"Would anyone like to volunteer to demonstrate how it feels to walk with both of these canes?"

The students looked at me, lifeless.

One stocky boy said, "Yeah, I'll do it."

"Great. Remind me of your name."

"Jeremy."

"Jeremy, please walk the length of the room and back using this aluminum cane in your left hand. Try not to rely on your left foot. Walk like you would if you had a badly sprained left ankle." I put the crook into his meaty palm, and he leaned on it with most of his weight.

Jeremy played a perfect part, limping down the center aisle, almost strutting. There were three rows of desks on either side of the aisle, facing one another. When my model student meandered back down the aisle, I switched the canes.

"Now try this one."

Again, he walked.

"OK, Jeremy, will you tell the class which cane would be easier to use if your ankle were injured?"

"Yeah. The one with four legs was a lot easier. More solid, I guess. The wooden one kinda wobbled."

"Thanks. Please take your seat. You are going to be seeing this wooden cane a lot this year, because I use it to walk. I will not be using it in the classroom, so when you see it hanging on this whiteboard tray, I expect you to leave it alone. A lot of times you will see students around the school staring at me and at this cane. In fact, as long as we are all staring at it right now, I might as well use it to teach you something about how this classroom is going to run. Write the word *cane* vertically on a piece of paper, please."

Nobody moved.

"Get out a piece of paper."

Nothing.

"Did anybody bring paper or pencils?"

Silence. They looked at one another, smirking.

"*Nobody* has paper?"

"No, miss. This is the first day of school," one kid offered. "No teacher has you doing any work on the first day. Everybody knows that."

"Fine. Use these." I grabbed the coffee can filled with unsharpened yellow pencils from my desk and passed it around, along with a brand-new pack of paper. I realized my class period was draining away as I watched students slowly move forward in the pencil-sharpening line, pushing one another and laughing as they waited.

Bad idea. What now, Ms. Maples?

When half of the students were back at their desks, I said, "That's enough. That's enough. The rest of you, just sit back down and look on with the person sitting next to you. I want to pick up where we left off. Please write *cane* vertically on your paper ..."

"Miss, I ain't got no pencil, yet," someone said.

"Yes, I know. We are going ahead anyway. Scoot your desk over and look on with your neighbor, please." He had been waiting for this command, of course. His neighbor was a cute blonde. He put his arm around her and pressed his lips to her ear, whispering something inappropriate that made her giggle.

I pointed at him. "Hey, watch it. And you don't need to sit *so* close. You knew what I meant when I told you to scoot over." He inched away from her, smacking his gum and grinning at me. He winked.

Somebody's cell phone rang.

"Don't answer that! Everyone, we are going to think about our class in terms of a walking cane. A cane supports you. There will be times when you, as an individual, will be too weak to walk on your own. If we create a classroom environment that is comfortable and supportive, then you will be able to lean on us. Follow the acrostic CANE down your paper as you write: COURTESY, ACCEPTANCE, NEATNESS, and EFFICIENCY." I wrote the words on the board, waiting for the few students who were writing.

"This is what we need in our classroom. We all saw Jeremy walk and heard him say that a cane with four-prongs is more stable. From now on, I want you to think of *courtesy* and *acceptance* as the two prongs, or principles, that dictate how we relate to one another, and *neatness* and *efficiency* as the two principles that dictate how we approach our work. Four prongs make a stable classroom environment that everyone can safely lean on. Does everybody get it?" I turned away from the dry-erase board and back to face the class. I was stunned. One student reclined, his sweatshirt hood low over his eyes. Several other students slept cozily, their heads brazenly resting on their desks.

"Excuse me! We are in *school*!" I raised my voice. "This is school, not your bedroom. Do you hear me? Do you get the analogy I am making, here? About the cane?"

The "ace of spades" raised his hand.

"Yes ..." Sighing, I searched my seating roster. "Um ... Matt. Do you want to say something about the CANE acrostic, Matt?"

"Yeah. Are you going to tell us why you walk like that?"

Several kids laughed.

I gritted my teeth. "I might, Matt, but I wouldn't say that I know you well enough, yet. Would you?"

The bell rang, and the entire class bolted. On the way out the door, I saw almost every student crumple the paper in a wad and toss it in the trash can, shouting to students passing in the hallway as they entered the stream.

"Hey!" I called after them. "Don't forget to bring your pencils tomorrow! See you then, everyone! Remember to bring your pencils!"

Of course, nobody did.

33

A HIGH SCHOOL TEACHER'S ROOKIE YEAR is fraught with tension—pitched on a sea of three parts misery, one part beauty. The maritime journey that began with courage and heart turns into a fierce storm; the teacher ends up blindly clinging to the steering wheel on a sodden deck, soaked to the skin, and praying for just one day of clear skies and full sails.

During my first year of teaching, I tripped and fell to my face on the sidewalk, just as a yellow bus pulled up to the school. My knee was bloody, and my books and papers took to the wind. The bus doors opened, and dozens of kids hurried past me, stepping over my purse and my shoe, until one Good Samaritan in the freshman class stopped to help me stand and pick up my things in time for me to get to my classroom before the bell.

During my first year of teaching, I did not let Austin go to the bathroom right when he urgently waved his arm in the air, but politely asked him to wait just ten more minutes. *Five* minutes later, I was scrubbing vomit from the carpet before my next class came in.

During my first year of teaching, my feet were so swollen they would hardly fit into my shoes.

During my first year of teaching, I fell in the hallway just before the second period bell rang and had to crawl on my hands and knees in a suit, so that I could pull myself up on a nearby doorknob before a student mob flooded from the classroom doors.

During my first year of teaching, Layla refused to take her final exam, and when I whispered to her that she had no choice in the matter, she unzipped her hoodie to display a T-shirt that read F—— YOU. I sent her to the office with a discipline referral. One of the assistant principals sent her back to my room with a Slinky.

"What are you doing back in here? I sent you to the office!" I said.

"He told me that if I kept my hoodie zipped up and just played with the Slinky quietly, I did not have to take the exam," Layla retorted.

When I called that assistant principal from the telephone in my classroom, he confirmed her story. Just like that, he had disempowered me. For the rest of the period, kids snickered as she smirked and poured that Slinky from palm to palm with a metallic *zing-zing-zing*! There was nothing I could do.

During my first year of teaching, I gave a culminating Artist's Eye Award to Trevor because of his incredible photojournalism projects. I should have known something was amiss when the kids started laughing and slapping him on the shoulders. At the end of the school day, he came back into my room and cried, confessing that he had never taken a single photograph for my class. He had borrowed and cheated since assignment one. Not only that, he had bragged to friends every day about his cunning charade and my idiocy. When I awarded him, his heart broke.

During my first year of teaching, I did not find the teachers' lounge or the English department workroom (filled with workbooks, helpful overhead transparencies to use, teaching guides, and word games) until January. No one, not even my assigned mentor, had told me such a place existed.

During my first year of teaching, Morgan argued with me, standing on her desk, calling me vulgar expletives, and throwing her mammoth literature textbook at me before running out of the door. I ducked the book, fighting tears and trying to direct the awed class back to their work—which suddenly seemed meaningless.

During my first year of teaching, my assigned district mentor was shocked by my daily slew of foolish mistakes: My classroom key got stuck in the lock *while* it was on a short lanyard around my neck. He teased meanly. I misspelled a word in my instructions on the board. He laughed. I actually warned a student that I had found a note that mentioned she had weed in her locker, so by the time an administrator asked her to reveal its contents, she was clean. My mentor chastised mercilessly. I strung the LCD projector cords right across the path from my desk to the podium and tripped on them, landing in a terrible sprawl.

"Why would you do something so *stupid*?" he asked incredulously.

I spent the last few minutes of my conference period crying as I wrote an e-mail to my mother, detailing my great dissatisfaction with my mentor's mistreatment of me all year. I told her he had called me "stupid." Then I accidentally sent the e-mail to *him* instead of her. So, basically, I proved him right. We were both called to the principal's office, and there we mutually ended our professional relationship.

During my first year of teaching, a student I had frequently overlooked, because of his shy and quiet demeanor, suddenly died of a heart attack while at home. At the funeral, his mother told me that mine was the only class he had ever come home talking about, smiling and sharing news about our latest activities. "He said you were the best teacher he'd ever had. He could not wait for me to meet you, Ms. Maples. I just never expected I'd be doing it *here*." The day after the funeral, as I stood behind the classroom podium, I happened to glance over to his empty desk and broke down crying in the middle of class. Most of the other students did not even know his name.

During my first year of teaching, I discovered that some of my fourth-period students were hungry because they could not afford lunch and were too embarrassed to fill out free-and-reduced-lunch applications. So I started buying a bag of apples to keep in a basket at the back of my room. The entire five-pound bag was empty within minutes every day. I brought in a new bag each morning. The students crunched their apples and leaned forward on an elbow, paying attention in class for the first time because they were fed.

During my first year of teaching, I continued my commitment to share gifts I have received by resurrecting my own crummy plastic academic trophies from junior high. I gave a Student of the Day Award at the beginning of class, putting one of the trophies on a student desk just for that hour. One time when the final bell rang, all the kids filed out, but Kenny stayed in his seat, staring at the small trophy. He remained with his face lowered and the award clutched in his fingers. He was a senior who had never heard his name called for an honor in school. "When you called my name"—he choked—"my legs almost went numb. This may be the only award I'll ever get. I am almost afraid to let it go."

During my first year of teaching, Jeremy came into class one day, infuriated. He hit the wall with a fist as he entered. "Will you cover me in the office if I tear someone up, Ms. Maples?" he asked.

"No, of course not," I answered. "What is the problem?"

The varsity defensive lineman grunted and threw his books on the desk as he sat down. "Some guys were making fun of the way you walk at lunch today. I wanted to rip them apart. They were messing with my favorite teacher."

During my first year of teaching, Kevin, an awkward senior in my creative writing elective course, wrote me a letter. He penned an unforgettable closing, "Ms. Maples, you make outcasts like me walk like kings among men."

During my first year of teaching, I cried both hopeless and joyful tears, enough tears to fill a Texas panhandle stock tank. I almost quit. It is hard to describe the gravitational force of the classroom, however. I deliberated endlessly that summer.

What if I can become a better teacher? What if I can help a student when no one else can?

As ocean waves return to their watery birthplace after cresting and breaking on the beach, I did not remain ruined ashore. When the new school year started, I returned.

By the pull of the tide, by the pull of the moon, waters swept me back on the open sea.

HOPE IS A ROLLER COASTER WE ARE INVITED to ride, not a train with a clear destination and a straight track. When we leave the platform to join other Hope riders, the only thing we know for sure is that there will be breathtaking climbs and heartbreaking falls. We also know we are going to come back around to the same platform we left, but we will be different, more alive, for the journey. Though we are unaware, throughout the whole ride we are completely safe. We feel as though our stomachs are leaving us. We feel as though we are slamming into walls. We hover above our seats during a drop, but we are safe. This is because Faith partners with Hope.

Faith operates as a seat belt and buckles us in, fastening across our hearts and keeping us secure. Whatever may happen, we will not fall. Hope only *seems* dangerous. It is not as life threatening as we would believe on most days. Besides, where Hope and Faith reside, Love is standing near. In fact, Love is sending us from that platform. And Love will be waiting for us when we make our brake-squealing and breathless return. It is undeniable. Hope is the ride we were meant to take.

Still we hesitate to board because we feel foolish, juvenile. We do not want to face disappointment *again*. We are afraid it might be the end of us. We question Hope's usefulness in the long run. We have given up on Faith, on Hope, on Love, or on all three.

During the sweltering summer between my first and second year of teaching, I realized that the quintessential element missing from my students' lives was Hope. The roller-coaster's platform was littered with loitering teenagers: children of drug addicts and parolees; students who were the adolescent parents of toddlers; students who had been called "special ed" so many times they began to think it was a synonym for *brainless*; students who had grown up poor, whose parents had grown up poor, and whose grandparents had grown up poor.

The ones who were from middle-class backgrounds did not have better prospects. Many had long bellied up to the bar of mediocrity, swallowing the same elixir some of their parents had ingested: a jigger of Just-Good-Enough. A report card riddled with low Bs and high Cs? That's not *really good*, but it is *just good enough* to avoid being grounded and having your car keys taken away. They did not have any goals. Hope's roller coaster had come around a few times, but neither the economically disadvantaged nor the financially average student had ever had the fortitude to board.

"Keep hope alive by living with intention!" I had effused that first year, introducing them to Henry David Thoreau and quoting from *Walden* on occasion. "Guys, we have to learn 'to live deliberately.' Whatever we choose to do with our lives, we need to exist artistically at heart. Thoreau got it right when he said, 'To affect the quality of the day, that is the highest of arts'!"

"What is the point of hoping and living deliberately?" they had questioned blandly. "Nothing ever changes. Nothing ever will."

Toward the end of my rookie year, three students from my two-hundred-student roster dropped out. *Three* of my dear students dropped out during their *sophomore* year. They had barely begun their education when they decided to end it. *One-and-a-half percent.* The statistic only seems small.

In truth, it was a tank I was willing to stand in front of in Tiananmen Square.

Therefore, skills in the subject of English language arts notwithstanding, I began my second year with a new curriculum in my briefcase: Hope. It had not been enough to lecture to my students about having hope and about living deliberately. I needed to stop talking about it and start modeling it. Some of my students had never seen Hope in action, I realized. Yet, I had built my entire life with the stones of small goals. I knew exactly how it felt to practice hope, and I was sure I could show my students how to do it. It occurred to me that it had been a few years since I had developed a plan for achieving a goal. Maybe it was time to go for it again. Maybe it was time to illustrate Hope through a teenager's preferred method of receiving information: in vivid color. Reality.

"Good morning!" I beamed on the students at the dawn of the 2004–05 semester. "My name is Ms. Maples, and you are in sophomore English. The first two things you need to know about me are: one, this is my second year of teaching, and two, I am what you would call a Big Nobody. But I have a goal. I have a goal and I mean to achieve it. Before you graduate in two years, I am going to shake the hand of the president of the United States,

George W. Bush." The students laughed at me, and a few rolled their eyes. Several looked at the clock.

"No normal lady gets to meet the president, miss. Hate to break it to you," a girl with dark-penciled eyebrows warned.

This was exactly what I wanted to hear. It was essential that I pick a goal that they thought was unattainable. It had to be a goal that was out of reach but close enough to brush against with the tips of our fingers. It probably would not happen. But ... it *could* happen, right?

I was not sure how I was going to do it, but in that moment, I knew I had to.

"You think I'm kidding. I have checked into this, you see. There are a couple of ways I could go about meeting the president. The most direct way I have found is to become a state Teacher of the Year. There are about three hundred thousand public school teachers in Texas. So, all I have to do is get noticed. Did I mention that this is only my second year of teaching?"

Again, my new students guffawed.

"What?" I laughed with them. "What? Come on! Do you doubt me? Do you think this is something I can't do in just two years?"

A tall boy named Eric, whose legs stretched out far into the aisle, said in a raspy voice, "No way, miss. Just sayin'. *No. Way.*"

"You don't think I can be noticed as I float in such a vast sea of veteran educators?"

"Well, how does someone win state Teacher of the Year anyway?" a girl sat up straight, interested.

"Glad you asked!" I glowed. "After initial recognition by fellow teachers as campus Teacher of the Year, the winner writes an essay. If the essay moves on to the finalist round at the district level, there is a panel interview. If the teacher is selected as district Teacher of the Year, then the essay moves on to the regional level. If the essay itself propels the teacher to win regional Teacher of the Year, then the essay moves on to the state level ..."

"*Essay, essay, essay!*" someone interrupted, mocking.

"Well, I'm an English teacher, so you know I love essays!" I continued.

"Watup, *esse!*" a Latino student shouted.

"Give me a break!" I laughed. "Come on, let me finish. If the state judges are impressed with the essay—e-s-s-a-y—then the teacher is invited to a panel interview as one of the state finalists. If the teacher soars during the interview, then that teacher is awarded the state title. So, there you go."

Everybody roared in amusement.

"Essays and confident self-expression are what an English teacher knows best." I smiled widely, using my hands to pretend a cartoon star was shining off my teeth. "Ching!"

The students laughed along with me.

"Writing and speaking happen to be two vital components of the sophomore language arts curriculum. Both are skills I employ fairly well and can teach you to do well, if you like. The best way I can teach you, in fact, is if we work together. Why learn by doing empty individual assignments, when we can tackle a real project together?"

They looked skeptical. "For real?"

"Yeah, for real. Do you still think it's impossible for me to meet the president?"

"Yes," the class said in unison, nodding and looking at one another.

"So, if it's impossible, you *don't* think I should go for it?"

"Again, no way!" Eric laughed and received light applause.

"Good," I said, winking. Then I turned and pinned a portrait of George and Laura Bush, both in blue jeans and leaning on a fence at the ranch, on my corkboard. "Watch closely. I'll show you what it means to believe in the impossible." Then I passed out the syllabus and discussed academic requirements, as I would on any normal first day of a language arts course. I did not mention the presidential goal again, but a picture of the First Couple hung front and center in my classroom as a symbol of my willingness to hope, bald-faced and unabashedly. I wanted my students to watch me get on the roller coaster and buckle up, unafraid to lose. My real goal was to see them follow suit.

This was not the only way I incorporated the concepts of hope and perseverance into my classroom. I used whatever I could. Sometimes, teachers must incorporate their own life experiences in order to capture imaginations. Learning always begins on an emotional level, in the heart. If a student is going to be coaxed into a posture of scholarship, they must first be engaged in spirit. I knew I had to inspire my students to maximize their shortcomings until weaknesses became strength, so I began using my own mobility limitations as effective teaching tools. My disability was not something to disguise but to utilize.

I had resumed physical therapy that year and was wearing thick plastic leg braces with enormous steel hinges. They *chinked* like spurs as I walked down the hall. They were painful too. My students often heard me sighing as I knelt down to rub my shins.

One day in the middle of class, a student whined that he was tired of trying to improve his reading by working through the comprehension strategies I taught.

"I'm done," he announced, tossing his unfinished book to the carpet. "Done." He was giving up.

A few other students threw down books and voiced their agreement. I had to work fast. Instinctively, I dropped to one knee and seized the teaching moment.

"My legs hurt, and I'm tired of these!" I began unstrapping my leg braces with dramatic flair. My students came alive!

"What are you doing, Ms. Maples? You can't stop wearing your leg braces if you want to get better!" They almost yelled, "You *can't* quit now!"

I smiled, raising my eyebrows. "Neither can you."

Their faces flushed with understanding as they returned to their novels. The boy who had quit first picked his book off the floor last.

Surely students respond to such a genuine attempt to connect. In order to be outstanding, a teacher must educate on a deeply personal level. Talented teachers seek appropriate ways to draw students into the mystery of learning, and they never relent on the process.

In late winter, when our entire campus prepared for an intense time of training for the upcoming state standardized test, I had an idea to improve our writing performance schoolwide. Our journalism students filmed and produced the daily announcements, then broadcast them through televisions mounted high in the corners of every classroom. I could not resist dipping my hands back into mass communications.

"Why aren't we using these TVs to teach English?" I asked

the other teachers during an English department meeting. "If I write a five-episode series of clever commercials that advertise essay-writing tips, would you guys join me in acting out roles?" Everyone agreed.

Stage fright set in when it came to the day of filming, however. I had the scripts and props in my room and had to star in four out of five of the commercials myself, because the other teachers backed out at the last minute. I was exasperated but felt that the commercials would benefit the students, so I forged ahead.

Every day for a week, two thousand students watched me act silly on the recorded announcements.

"Never start an essay with the words, 'I think!' *I think* stinks," I crowed, spraying air freshener all around me.

"Poor grammar leads to confusing sentences that give the reader a headache! *Editing: the Headache Medicine.*" I held a pill bottle filled with jelly beans close to my face and offered a saccharine grin.

As a result of the commercials, kids all over the school got excited about writing ... well, as excited as a teenager gets about schoolwork. A few dropped by to introduce themselves to me and to tell me that they remembered the slogans during their last essay for another class. They thought the tips might have helped a little bit.

Most of the two hundred faculty and staff members who had never met me suddenly had a face to put with the name. Of course, it was unintentional on my part, but those videos put me in the limelight. When the Teacher of the Year ballots landed in our boxes the following month, my colleagues chose me along with another teacher.

Our principal came on the PA system and created some suspense before announcing the names of the two 2005 Fossil Ridge High School Teachers of the Year. All my students were looking at me, waiting. I played along with the game.

"This could be it! Here's hoping I am on my way to state!" I said, crossing my fingers and smiling broadly.

The principal said the other teacher's name first and then mine. I had not believed it really would happen. I doubled over in my desk chair, screaming. My whole class was jumping and screaming too. A junior varsity soccer player recorded the whole scene on his camera phone. When he replayed it for us, we laughed even harder at ourselves.

The next day, the public relations officer for my district sent me the form for the state application, which is a thirteen-page essay required at the district level too.

"Time to get to work on some serious writing!" I bubbled to my students. For once, the thought of working on an essay did not elicit groans from all around the room. This essay was different. It was the one we had been waiting for. Over the next two weeks, I would pass out copies of certain sections, and students would edit away (not that I applied many of their sophomoric changes, of course). I would read aloud portions, and we would discuss the style and word choice I had employed.

To help me practice for the panel interview, each student chose paper strips from a basket I had filled with several hundred common education interview questions. From my perch on a bar stool at the front of the room, I answered question after question during the last five minutes of class every day. Though I had not said a word about interviewing etiquette or personal poise, my students understood the components of good communication the moment they became interviewers themselves. It was a teacher's perfect opportunity: a learning exercise in disguise.

"You should smile more. Say, 'Thanks for inviting me to come,' or something to start it off."

"You are shifting around in your seat, Ms. Maples. Sit still and quit bouncing your leg. You look nervous."

"That answer was pretty good, but you said 'um' way, way too many times. Next time, it would be better to think for a minute about your answer instead of figuring it out as you go along. You are stumbling around while you speak."

"I don't know a lot about teaching, but that answer sounded kinda corny to me. Not special. Kinda like what anybody would say."

"Miss, you're slouching."

"What was *that*? That answer was not clear at all. I had no idea what you meant. I'll ask it again, and you can start over."

"Great job on that round! Do it like that every time."

"We are going to win, miss." Eric nodded, leaning back, lacing long fingers behind his head, and winking at me. "We got this."

We are going to win. We.

It had become *our* award, our goal, our Hope. My heart almost stopped when I witnessed the transformation. My students were filing on board Hope's roller coaster after all.

My essay made the final round at the district level. The day before the panel interview, my students wrote encouragement notes on small Post-its and stuck them all over my desk. I bought a customizable travel coffee mug and lined all the notes under the plastic, as a sweet memento of our consolidated effort.

Later, the students who helped me edit my essay and prepare for the interview received the news from my own mouth: the district panel interview had been a shattering wreck. I had blubbered and cried the entire time, not a bit as composed as I had been throughout our practice sessions. They were consoling.

"It's okay, Ms. Maples. Shake it off. At least you tried."

But a few days later, the school-board president announced that I won district Teacher of the Year, to all our surprise. My students departed for the summer with hugs and tears.

If only Hope were a short process. The Spanish word for "hope" is *esperanza*. The word for "wait" is *esperar*. It seems perfect to me that the words are so similar. Hoping and waiting are nearly synonymous in any language, especially the language of the heart. Solomon acknowledges this in Proverbs 13:12, "Hope deferred makes the heart sick, but a longing fulfilled is a tree of life."

My district would not send my essay to the regional round until the following summer. So, those sophomores were seniors before they heard another word about it.

35

THE REGION XI TEACHER OF THE YEAR nominees and their guests gathered that autumn at the Petroleum Club in a Fort Worth high-rise. While other district candidates from ten counties in north central Texas inched their way past the ice sculpture at the glittering buffet table, I stood at the floor-to-ceiling windows, gazing out over the Cowtown skyline. I mentally noted the streets and buildings that I recognized. The only significant structure I could *not* see was HealthSouth, my old rehabilitation hospital from thirteen years earlier. Still looking, I followed the highway with my eyes, until it left my line of vision, looping the south side of the city like a latigo. I could not see the hospital grounds from the direction I was facing. The literal picture touched my heart. HealthSouth, it seemed, was behind me.

After a pleasant dinner, someone from Region XI read a portion from the essays of the 2006 elementary and secondary winners before announcing their names.

The dinner guests were silent when she began, "In 1994, I bought a pair of running shoes for my twentieth birthday ..."

My mother was sitting at my table that evening. I glanced at her as she lowered her gaze; a tear fell to her lap.

When I walked up to the stage to receive the bouquet of red roses and the crystal award, my principal had to help me climb the small set of stairs. My balance had responded to the emotion of the evening by becoming even shakier than usual.

They asked me to say a brief word of acceptance. It was my first time to take a podium in front of a crowd that large, and I was nervous. I said only, "Sometimes people read negative things in the news and wonder if there is any hope for public schools. Is there hope? You can *bet* on it."

My students had been so right not to think of it as my award alone. But it was not exactly ours either. The only One who had done anything was God. Without Him, I would still be lying in a vegetative state. Worse, yet, I would be dead. All anyone has to do is read Acts 17:24–28 to know that our lives are not accidents.

The God who made the world and everything in it is the Lord of heaven and earth and does not live in temples built by hands. And he is not served by human hands, as if he needed anything, because he himself gives all men life and breath and everything else. From one man he made every nation of men that they should inhabit the whole earth; and he determined the times set for them and the exact places where they should live. God did this so that men would seek him and perhaps reach out for him and find him, though he is not far from each one of us. "For in him we live and move and have our being."

My life is not my own. Because I have been told more than once that my time was up, there is a constant sense that every day is a small gemstone in my hand. Unexpected and lovely. I do not need much more than a new day to make me praise. Still, He gives more.

A week or two later, the district superintendent greeted me in the school cafeteria and gave me an oversized bouquet in front of everyone.

"You are one of three state finalists," he said. All the students at their tables dropped pizza and hamburgers and cheered.

My knees almost gave way.

There was not enough time to prepare for the interview. I continued with my regular lesson plans as if nothing new were happening. But I got out the old travel coffee cup lined in hand-written Post-it notes, and I sipped from my students' encouragement throughout the day.

The evening before the state interview, my mother and I started our drive to Austin around 7:00 PM. She was going to take the wheel while I took notes, trying to list some of the classroom stories that were most dear to me from the last four years of teaching. She helped by reminding me of a few she remembered me telling. The trip from Fort Worth to Austin should only take about three and a half hours. That night it took eight. The traffic was at a complete standstill, due to highway construction. We did not pull into the hotel until 3:00 AM. So much for looking fresh and prepared for an important interview. Lupus pain was atrocious the next morning from my having had little rest and exorbitant stress. It was all I could do to grit my teeth and drag myself into the commissioner's conference room at the Texas Education Agency. Even as I did, I was praying.

Lord, please do what is best. I do not want to move forward with this award if it will end up being a detriment to my health. I do not want anything to ruin the season of physical strength I have been enjoying. Please take care of my body.

Thirteen judges sat around a long conference table. They indicated a chair at the head of the table, what seemed like miles from the other end. I wore a pink blazer with a thin pink belt. Underneath, I wore a black T-shirt that looked like a simple shell from the front. On the back of the T-shirt, underneath the blazer, were the gold letters I had paid a team jersey shop to iron on at the opening of football season. I wore it regularly as a Fossil Ridge fan. The T-shirt bore the name and number of one of my current students who played wide receiver. I looked pulled together like a representative of educators on the outside, but underneath, I was just the teacher who sat on aluminum bleachers and cheered for touchdowns on Friday nights. I wanted to remind myself from the beginning of the interview to the end that my choice to become a teacher was all about encouraging young people.

After that tense panel interview, I walked out of the brooding 1970s Texas Education Agency building and into the fresh air, facing the coral granite state capitol in panoramic view a few blocks away.

"This recognition doesn't really matter," I whispered to myself. "I am doing exactly what I am supposed to be doing with my life."

The October temperature was brisk, and even the rustling

burnt orange leaves seemed to know it was a Longhorn Saturday. University of Texas tailgate parties lined the streets like state-fair booths. The aroma of charcoal and grilled hamburgers rode on the breeze. Looking up, I smiled. God had brought me so far. So far. I hurried to the hotel to change clothes before heading back to Texas Memorial Stadium to attend the football game, still the same old teacher, now thrilled to see one of her former students play wide receiver at the college level.

A week later, the kids were taking a literature test when the telephone rang.

"Ms. Maples, are you in the middle of class?" said the commissioner of education, with a Texas twang as thick as a patch of prickly pears.

"Yes, ma'am. They are taking a test right now." I looked around the room to see every pencil down and every eye trained on me as I paced and talked. "Or *not* taking it, as the case may be."

She laughed.

"Ms. Maples, you tell those kids to put down that test for good." She paused before continuing, "I am calling today to tell them that their teacher has been recognized by the state as the 2007 Texas Secondary Teacher of the Year!"

The students exploded.

Within hours, the district superintendent visited to congratulate me, and my principal made an announcement to the entire campus. Teachers ran up to hug me and ask questions. Television and newspaper reporters were filming and snapping photographs before the day ended.

But of all the visitors who came by that day, the most meaningful were the seniors who had helped me work on that first essay during their sophomore year. I will always be grateful that most of them were right there on campus to hear the announcement.

"We won!" one of them shouted, enveloping me in warm hug. "We really won!"

After all is said and done, it would seem that Hope had won.

Two weeks later, I traveled to Austin again to receive the award formally at a banquet attended by VIPs from the Texas Education Agency, the other state finalists, and regional teachers of the year. I gave my first speech as a Texas Teacher of the Year:

A reporter recently asked me to relay the most rewarding aspect of teaching. I told him that leading students into a lifetime of wise choices is most rewarding to me.

"The teenagers I teach are facing some critical decisions," I told him. "They are confronted with underage drinking, drugs, violence, shoplifting, reckless driving, and other situations that affect our community. Good teachers inspire their students to evaluate possible outcomes, weighing choices made deliberately against choices made impulsively."

He took a step back and said, "Why don't you just stick to teaching English? Isn't that what you were hired to do? What right have you to become involved in their lives, even indirectly, through guiding them in decision-making? Who are you to define morality?"

This reporter doesn't know that on Tuesday I took up a note from one of the brightest and most enthusiastic students in my class, and that it contained blatant references to his use of cocaine. This reporter doesn't know that on Wednesday I handed an administrator a student essay entitled "Bangin' Blue" in which a fifteen year old confessed that he is ready to kill a man in order to become a member of the Crips gang. This reporter doesn't know that during our last research project over ethics in the workplace, my students overwhelmingly agreed that there is no such thing as a lie, because something is true if you want it to be true badly enough. That stealing is okay if the person you are stealing from is someone you don't know or if that person is richer than you. That beating or even killing someone is not wrong if the person deserved it.

If I teach them how to write a complete sentence or how to analyze literature, and that's *all* I teach them ... have I really done my job?

How can I teach Robert Frost's classic poem, for example, without applying its closing lines to their lives:

Two roads diverged in a wood, and I—
I took the one less traveled by,
And that has made all the difference.

"This poem is not about roads!" I tell my class, "It is about choices. What you do today affects tomorrow!"

World War III is already underway. It is not on distant shores; it is as far away as the curb. For some of you with teenagers of your own, it may be as far away as the bedroom down the hall. Parents of the very young: you will be called to the front lines sooner than you think. We are fighting for our children. They are losing a sense of society. If you have not reread the classic *Lord of the Flies* since your high school days, I highly recommend that you take another look at the reasons why we need to foster a healthy community for our children's sake.

If teachers offer only core content, our lessons are skeletons without muscle. It is where content and character meet that we engage the learner, giving movement and life to what we say. We bring more than just our minds into the classroom. We bring our hearts.

Students come to us with all kinds of wounds, some potentially fatal to their success. Our classrooms are intensive care units, and we are the academic physicians. We must never remove educational life support. We must never give up or stop caring. Without the component of caring, a classroom is just a room. Without the component of caring, a teacher is just a bystander. For a few students, one dedicated teacher can mean the difference between a lifetime of paralysis or truly moving forward.

We cannot afford to be afraid to bring character into the classroom. The prognosis for many of our students is grim, indeed. We have to believe that there are grand stages waiting to receive them as this grand stage receives me today. Integrity will take them where they need to go. By upholding lives of virtue ourselves, by maintaining personal and professional standards, we illustrate the manner in which success is achieved. Not through the back door, but through the front.

Teachers cannot heal all wounds. But dreams will become reality for some of our students. And that is enough to keep us unlocking our classroom doors every Monday morning.

Just look at the marvelous work my teachers have wrought for me. Yes, I am a person with disabilities. But my outstanding teachers taught me to view myself as a person with possibilities.

And that has made all the difference.

36

FORT WORTH'S WARM RED-BRICK STREETS became a trampoline that bounced me to Houston and back, to Austin and back, to Dallas and back, even to Louisiana and back, again and again during my year of service to the state. My cane hung from the edge of countless podiums as I spoke before school districts, universities, and educational organizations. I felt like a quarterback encouraging an entire team of Texas educators. But even with my incredible opportunities, there was one thing missing.

I never shook the hand of the president.

Texas, in all its legendary "bigness," has two state teachers of the year—elementary and secondary—not just one, like most of the other states. Only *one* teacher from each state is permitted to visit the White House to meet the president. Early in my service year, I learned that only the 2007 Texas Elementary Teacher of the Year would be representing the state of Texas at the Rose Garden ceremony. My heart was broken. I would only be going to Washington D.C. that weekend to attend the National Teacher of the Year conference with my award-winning colleagues, not to attend the other exciting events. Only fifty-six teachers—a representative from each of the fifty states, plus the Virgin Islands, the Northern Mariana Islands, Puerto Rico, the Department of Defense, American Samoa, and the District of Columbia—would have a seat in the Rose Garden. There was not a second spot for Texas. Now, someone should explain to me why there is a shortage of chairs in Washington. I even promised not to say a word and only drink water.

"Is there *no way?*" I begged the national program coordinators.

"We understand your disappointment," they said. "Unfortunately, the decision is nonnegotiable."

"But ..."

"We're sorry. It is not possible for you to attend the White House events with us this week."

What a ruthless blow.

I did not want any of the other luminous opportunities as state Teacher of the Year as much as I wanted to meet President Bush. In fact, that was the *only* prospect I had wanted at all. Just like my students predicted, shaking the hand of the president was impossible.

Disappointment quickly turned into jealousy. On the day of the Rose Garden ceremony, I sulked in my Virginia hotel room, watching TV with a delivery pizza in my lap and tears in my eyes. Exclusion hurts just as much in your thirties as it does in middle school.

Anyone would have guessed that after having been delivered from life as an invalid, I would have a buoyant and indestructible faith. I am ashamed to say that I could not stop being upset that easily. It is not as if we can learn all the lessons there are to learn about ourselves and about God at one time. It would be nice if every one of the tests of our character and integrity came in exactly the same form each time. Then we could recognize what was coming and batten down the hatches for the bluster that would knock us off keel, even in our finest moments.

Beware, Cinderella.

Discontentment and Envy are your ugly stepsisters.

When any of us look hard enough, we can find plenty of reasons to pout. Even at the dreamiest palace ball. My mother was exactly right when she intimated that there would never be an end to desire.

"There will always be one more inch to move," she had said.

Listen to one who was once motionless on a mat: it is the truth. There is always another inch.

My broken relationship with my father is another one of those areas I wish would budge. God is still bringing me through the continued effort of handling that hurt. My father hardly acknowledged my professional achievement as state Teacher of the Year, much less attended any of the congratulatory events for me. I have given hundreds of keynote addresses, but he has not heard one of them. Ironically, this ongoing wound has helped me realize an essential component of dealing with relational crises: we can never do enough to win someone back.

Yes, I have forgiven him. That has never changed through passing years. However, now I can admit that, in the back of my mind, I had kept a towering expectation in view. I could not help hoping that one day my father would be so proud of my accomplishments that he would *run* to claim me as his own. I was sure of it.

When I won Texas Teacher of the Year, and he did not run, I dropped my hands in despair.

"I can't do more than this," I said. "In my field, there is nothing more laudatory than state Teacher of the Year. But it did not make him want me."

What do we do? We can remain open to reconciliation with our loved ones. We should pray for our loved ones. We must forgive our loved ones. But we cannot try to earn them.

Within this painful realization, there is freedom, because we finally rest from our striving to earn affection and let God handle the situation without our help. Who knows what He will do. I pray that surrender brings you—brings all of us—a lovely surprise.

The same desire to surrender motivated me to drop "the president issue," which was the disenchanting dent in my royal carriage. I purposed to enjoy every moment of that marvelous year, which came to an end far too quickly. Before I knew it, all the opportunities were over.

God has a different definition of "over" than we do.

I taught another year of high school English after my spring semester sabbatical as Texas Teacher of the Year, then moved to sixth-grade language arts at another campus in my district. Just when I thought I had returned to the front of the classroom, I found I was the student. God was teaching me the most important lesson of all: that perseverance and patience are an essential part of any goal-setting curriculum.

In the spring of 2010, my high school alma mater invited me to attend their annual fund-raising dinner, always a semiformal event with an entertaining keynote speaker. Several weeks before the event, a cameraman visited my classroom to capture a few shots of me teaching for a recruiting video for the school. He interviewed me about the private school and how it influenced me and prepared me for a career. For a brief moment, I talked about being Texas Teacher of the Year. Of course, I told a little bit about my goal to meet the president and that I had missed out on shaking his hand.

Though it had been exactly three years since I was excluded from the Rose Garden ceremony, I could not help but revisit my disillusionment. President Bush was going to be the speaker at that dinner.

Could this finally be my chance to shake his hand? Hope welled up again. With great bravado, I asked the secretary to the president of my alma mater if I might have a moment to meet President Bush and thank him for his service to our country during the days of our great national distress and sense of vulnerability.

"Security will be too tight," she said. "You are going to have to be content just to breathe the same air as the president. Shaking his hand is impossible."

And I finally admitted that it was.

That night, I dismissed a final wave of disappointment as I zipped up my gray satin cocktail dress and smoothed on lip gloss. I was determined to enjoy every minute of that evening. I was happy. I did not need another inch.

Finding my assigned table in the farthest corner on the front row of tables, I sat in the shadows, glad to have an unobstructed view of the podium.

When they introduced the president, he and his Secret Service entourage walked in through a door very close to my table. The *instant* he crossed the threshold into the dining room, he looked me in the eye. For a moment, I lost my breath. Then he winked. I looked around.

Did he just wink or was it my imagination? Had it really been at me? Is this one of those cases when you wave back at someone in a grocery store, only to have that person run right past you to greet someone else who is standing behind you?

But I was *sure* he was looking at me.

Something on his face had said, "Get ready, kid."

The ovation settled down, and I took my seat and sighed. That is when the big screen lit up with my face. I froze. The clips the cameraman filmed of me explaining my presidential goal played suddenly in front of one thousand people. Wide-eyed with surprise, I sat up as straight as a meerkat. A voice hammered over the microphone, "Nika Maples, the forty-third president of the United States, George W. Bush, invites you to join him at the head table for dinner this evening."

I was almost shocked into paralysis again.

I could barely make it through the crowd without collapsing, I was crying so hard. Even though I was escorted, the trip across the hotel dining room seemed like a trip across the vast Sahara. I thought we would never get there.

When I saw him, my hand shot out, almost involuntarily. He ignored my gesture, reached up, and took my face into his hands. He held it there only a few seconds, but as he did, he looked at me with smiling eyes and a grin so big it became a hearty laugh. Then he hugged me and kissed me on the cheek.

For thirty minutes, one of the most powerful men of the twenty-first century charmed those of us sitting at his table with his wit and gentle humility. I was seated beside him. Our guest of honor acted as a gracious host, doing whatever he could to make us feel at ease.

When I was just sitting there, staring at my dinner plate in a giddy stupor, I did not notice that he was being a gentleman and waiting for me to begin. A couple of minutes passed, and he finally leaned over and whispered, "You are going to have to start eating, so that I can." We both laughed at my terrible case of nerves.

His easygoing nature disarmed all of us. He told some interesting stories and even talked about his latest golf game as if he were anyone having dinner with friends. Eventually, I warmed up and enjoyed the conversation. At one point, I told him that my favorite moment from my Texas Teacher of the Year experience was throwing out the first pitch at a Texas Rangers baseball game. I explained that, though I had practiced pitching the sixty-foot distance, standing on an actual MLB pitching mound in front of a crowd had been a completely different story. I knew my pitch would never make it, and I had almost panicked. Like lightning, I had dropped the ball to the grass and flipped my cane upside down. Then I had "putted" the ball to home plate with the crook of my cane.

He laughed and said, "I can relate to that! When I threw out the first pitch at Yankee Stadium after 9/11, Derek Jeter pulled me aside just before I took the mound. 'Watch out,' he warned me. 'If you bounce it, they'll boo ya.' I was lucky I made it to home plate, but listen, you and I *both* had a back-up plan. You had a cane. I had a bulletproof vest!"

Later, he grew somber for a moment, and his voice became quiet. "Tell me a little bit about living with lupus," he said tenderly, where only I could hear. Briefly, I told him that I had been quadriplegic and had learned to walk and talk again. "Are you mad about it sometimes?" he asked.

"Just thankful," I answered simply.

He nodded. "I guess we all can take a path of thankfulness or a path of bitterness when Life gives us an experience we do not want. You have chosen the better path. I'm proud of you for that, Nika."

At the end of the evening, he kissed me on the cheek again and said he enjoyed sitting beside me for dinner. He sincerely thanked me for teaching school and for sharing my story with him. It was obvious that he meant it.

As he stood to take the stage, he leaned over to me and smiled. "Bye, babe," he said with the familiarity Texans always share.

One word encompasses my overall impression of the forty-third president of the United States: *genuine.* He appeared to be thoroughly present in the moment, concentrating on making those around him feel welcomed and appreciated, instead of focusing on his own comfort. My aspiration would be to have the same deliberate depth, the same rich personality, the same expansive confidence.

After the closing remarks of the evening, the emcee dismissed the crowd, and a small group of close friends hurriedly gathered around me to ask questions. We lingered in the ballroom until every other guest had departed and all the tables and chairs were gone.

Except one.

I looked over a friend's shoulder. One by one, members of the waitstaff removed grimy aprons, straightened wilting bow ties, sat down, and posed for snapshots in the one chair that remained in the dining room: the president's chair. Each face glowed, smiling for the camera. I knew how they felt; I could not stop smiling either.

I would have missed one of the most incredible experiences of my life, if I had been invited to meet him in Washington for a quick handshake, as I had originally hoped. My hope was too small.

For the three years between the White House incident and my dinner with the president, I had been plagued with self-doubt—wondering what I had done wrong, what I could have changed, why I had come so close but missed the mark by a fraction of an inch.

Oh, but there is a miraculous internal dynamic that occurs when our longings are fulfilled, not by our own hands, but by the Lord's. Suddenly, our years of waiting and wondering become as insubstantial as vapor. His wisdom is sweet and so much better than our own that we find ourselves feeling we could have waited even longer, had we only known.

I pray that both you and I hold on to this as tightly as we are able ... the surety that everything—everything!—will be worth it. Even the suffering.

There are so many spiritual elements I do not understand. As the years go by, however, I think I understand suffering more and more. It is the one thing that pulls our hearts most closely to God's—for protection, for help, for relief, for comfort. It is the one thing that reminds us that we must not wander too far away.

In the book of Genesis, Jacob wrestled with God by the river, begging for blessing. Afterward, he limped. Yet his struggle itself was the blessing he sought because it deepened his relationship with the Lord. His lingering disability was the painful reminder of all he had been through in order to grow spiritually. He just would not let go of God. (See Genesis 32.)

We are like Jacob.

Sometimes we carry scars from gruesome emotional battles for the rest of our lives. Our wounds change us: the way we walk, the way we talk, even the way we perceive the world from then on. Though we are wrestle-weary, our pain is precious, because—hopefully—it has taught us more about the One who created us.

Do we have the faith in retrospect to see that our suffering had a purpose? Does the knowledge that He has a bigger plan affect the state of our faith during the fiery trial or struggle? Can we lean on God in such a way that we stop blaming Him when "bad things happen to good people" and start believing that He can make bad things result in our spiritual good?

These questions of belief span the width and breadth of our time on earth. We answer them again and again. We answer them on so many occasions because, throughout our lives, the Great Teacher is testing our faith to see if we really depend upon Him. Trials are a kind of spiritual assessment. "The *testing* of your faith develops perseverance," James 1:3 explains (emphasis mine). God already knows what is in our hearts, but He wants *us* to know too, and the only way to show us is to lay our hearts bare.

Trials are uncomfortable and inconvenient. Some are devastating, but even in the midst of them, we are ultimately safe. Never alone. On the contrary, when we are hurting, when we feel most vulnerable and frightened, that is when the Lord draws close.

In the classroom of life, there will be a test, whether we study for it or not. The Bible, our textbook, cannot remain unread if we expect to develop the skills we need to pass. When we are in the middle of a brutal spiritual assessment, God walks very near our desks and leans down with an encouraging countenance and a soft tone of voice. He places a warm hand on our shoulders and asks if we are prepared. Like every good teacher, he hopes that the most important lessons have been learned along the way. He wants to celebrate with us after the tests are finally over. Even so, we would do well to remember that life is not about making the grade.

It is about trusting our Teacher.

ACKNOWLEDGEMENTS

The hardest part of writing a memoir is not writing it, but living it. I extend my tender gratitude to the friends who walked beside me when I could not walk myself, especially Becky Jeffrey Brooks, Brian Huff, Emily Trice Macht, David Stotts, and Rob Thomas. Our laughter has been the best medicine.

I also want to acknowledge the work of countless specialists, particularly the rheumatologists, who cared for my health more than twenty years. I appreciate all of them.

Thank you to my first principal, Todd Tunnell, for seeing a capable teacher when he looked at the counseling assistant shredding paper in the back of the office. I am indebted to him for giving me his confidence and the keys to my first classroom.

If only I could carve a thank you note in granite to my friends and fellow Texas Teachers of the Year, Dana Boyd (2007), Barbara Dorff (2002), Jack Cody (2000), Linda Duffy (2001), and the marvelous Grant Simpson (2008). They are irreplaceable.

I am grateful to the educators and administrators from Fossil Ridge High School, Keller Independent School District,

Region XI, and the Texas Education Agency for giving me the opportunity of a lifetime.

Thank you to President George W. Bush, for his enduring example of graciousness. The evening I finally met him was one small dinner for a president, one giant dream for a teacher.

Words fail when I think of the impression left on this manuscript by Byron Williamson and Jeana Ledbetter. They fortified my rickety structure and added elegance. Thank you, thank you.

Heartfelt appreciation to Rick Atchley, for contributing to my faith by bringing me face-to-face with the Word of God for years and for extending spiritual guidance as an early reader. His advice significantly shaped my telling of this story.

Thank you to Helen Macdonald, Beth Plemons, and Christi Romeo for their gift with words and to Alan Hebel and Ian Simkoviak for their gift with design. Their expertise made it easy for me to trust them with something so precious to me.

Aunt Lisa, thank you for taking ten composition books and typing the first draft seventeen years ago! I have not forgotten that sweet gesture, or how I tried to hurry you. That is laughable now.

Sincere admiration to RJ Washington, who, when I told him I had put this manuscript in a drawer, looked me in the eye and told me to start doing what I was born to do. That day my student was my coach.

I cheerfully thank all of the early readers who trudged through the marsh of my words and offered genuine feedback and encouragement at various stages: Becky Brooks, Josh Dunford, Kelly Felps, Amy Howard, Sam Jeffrey, Mary Beth Petr, Brandon Scott Thomas, and Marla Wharton.

An outpouring of thanks to Terry Hudson, who has been an

advocate for me and for this book and who does not sit still when his heart is stirred.

My heart has seen the Eighth Wonder of the World in the unconditional love of Carol, Mark, and Tara Maples, who are not only my family but my closest friends. How can I repay you for your years of unflagging belief in me? You have battled in prayer and have refused to let me stay down. Thank you for your end-less laughter and for spending an entire day reading these pages aloud to me. That memory is of unspeakable worth.

Every word I have ever written is a thank you letter to God, who does not blink.